STAAR Grade 6 Mathematics Assessment Secrets

Study Guide
Your Key to Exam Success

STAAR Test Review for the
State of Texas Assessments of Academic Readiness

Dear Future Exam Success Story:

Congratulations on your purchase of our study guide. Our goal in writing our study guide was to cover the content on the test, as well as provide insight into typical test taking mistakes and how to overcome them.

Standardized tests are a key component of being successful, which only increases the importance of doing well in the high-pressure high-stakes environment of test day. How well you do on this test will have a significant impact on your future- and we have the research and practical advice to help you execute on test day.

The product you're reading now is designed to exploit weaknesses in the test itself, and help you avoid the most common errors test takers frequently make.

How to use this study guide

We don't want to waste your time. Our study guide is fast-paced and fluff-free. We suggest going through it a number of times, as repetition is an important part of learning new information and concepts.

First, read through the study guide completely to get a feel for the content and organization. Read the general success strategies first, and then proceed to the content sections. Each tip has been carefully selected for its effectiveness.

Second, read through the study guide again, and take notes in the margins and highlight those sections where you may have a particular weakness.

Finally, bring the manual with you on test day and study it before the exam begins.

Your success is our success

We would be delighted to hear about your success. Send us an email and tell us your story. Thanks for your business and we wish you continued success-

Sincerely,

Mometrix Test Preparation Team

TABLE OF CONTENTS

Numbers, Operations, and Quantitative Reasoning

Integer, percent, fraction, and decimal

An integer is a positive whole number, negative whole number, or zero; for example, 8 is an integer. A percent is a part per hundred; for example, 20% is 20 parts per hundred. A fraction is an expression where one number is being divided by another; for example, $\frac{20}{10}$ is a fraction. All rational numbers can be written as a positive or negative whole number, or zero, being divided by another positive or negative whole number. A decimal contains a whole number (or zero), which is to the left of the decimal point, and a portion of a whole number, which is to the right of the decimal point; for example, 20.53 is a number is decimal form. All rational numbers are either terminating decimals, where the numbers to the right of the decimal point end, or repeating decimals, where the numbers to the right of the decimal repeat in a pattern infinitely. Integers, percents, fractions, and decimals are all forms of rational numbers.

Rational numbers from least to greatest

Example
Order the following rational numbers from least to greatest: 12%, 1.2, $\frac{1}{12}$, 12.

From least to greatest: $\frac{1}{12}$, 12%, 1.2, 12.

Equivalent forms of rational numbers

Example 1
Convert each quantity below. Identify the form of each given quantity and describe the new form of the quantity.
a) Write 1 as a fraction.
b) Write 0.4 as a percent.

a) 1 is a whole number. A fraction is an expression where one number is being divided by another. To write a whole number as a fraction, write the whole number over the integer 1.
$$1 = \frac{1}{1}$$

b) 0.4 is a decimal. A percent is a part per hundred. To write a decimal as a percent, move the decimal place to digits to the right.
0.4 = 40%

Example 2
Convert each quantity below. Identify the form of each given quantity and describe the new form of the quantity.
a) Write $\frac{6}{2}$ as a decimal.
b) Write 200% as a whole number.

a) $\frac{6}{2}$ is a fraction. A decimal contains a whole number (or zero), which is to the left of the decimal point, and a portion of a whole number, which is to the right of the decimal point.

b) 200% is a percent. A whole number is a positive integer or zero. To write a percent as a whole number, first write the percent as a decimal. Move the decimal two places to the left.

200% = 2.00
If the quantity after the decimal is 0, then the number can be written as a whole number by only writing the whole number portion of the decimal.
2.00 = 2

Prime factorization

The prime factorization of a number is a number written as a multiple of prime numbers. A prime number is a number that is only divisible by itself and 1. For example, the prime factorization of 30 is: $2 \cdot 3 \cdot 5$, and the prime factorization of 40 is: $2 \cdot 2 \cdot 2 \cdot 5 = 2^3 \cdot 5$.

Factors, common factors, and greatest common factor

Example
The factors of a number are all integers by which the number can be divided.
Factors of 18: 1, 2, 3, 6, 9, 18
Factors of 24: 1, 2, 3, 4, 6, 8, 12, 24
Common factors are all factors that are shared by both integers. Common factors of 18 and 24 are: 1, 2, 3, and 6. The greatest common factor is the greatest factor by which 18 and 24 can both be divided: 6.

Multiples

A multiple of a number is product of the number and an integer.

Example 1
Find two multiples for both 27 and 25.

Examples of multiples of 27 and 25 are:
$27 \cdot 2 = 54$; $27 \cdot 10 = 270$
$25 \cdot 4 = 100$; $25 \cdot 3 = 75$

Example 2
Find the least common multiple of 45 and 66.

The least common multiple of two numbers can be found by first finding the prime factorization of number.
$45 = 3^2 \cdot 5$
$66 = 2 \cdot 3 \cdot 11$
The least common multiple of two numbers must contain the prime factors in both numbers, raised to the highest power in each prime factorization. The

least common factor of 45 and 66 would need to have a 2, a 3, to the second power, a 5, and an 11: $2 \cdot 3^2 \cdot 5 \cdot 11 = 990$

Diagram and equation to represent a fraction

Example
A pie is divided into 8 equal pieces. There are 5 pieces remaining. Draw a picture to determine what fraction of the pie is remaining if 2 additional pieces are eaten. Write an equation represented by the diagram.

Draw a circle, and divide the circle into 8 equal pieces. Shade 5 of the pieces to show the pieces remaining.

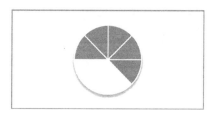

From the pieces remaining, two pieces are eaten. This can be symbolized by shading these two pieces differently.

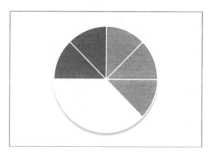

There are 3 of the original 8 pieces remaining, which is $\frac{3}{8}$ of the pie. This can be expressed with the equation: $\frac{5}{8} - \frac{2}{8} = \frac{3}{8}$.

Simplifying expressions

Example
a) $7.1 - \frac{3}{4}$
b) $\frac{6}{5} + 0.4$

a) To subtract fractions and decimals, first make sure that the numbers are the same form. The answer can be written as either a fraction or decimal. If using fractions, the fractions must have a common denominator.

$$7.1 - \frac{3}{4} = \frac{71}{10} - \frac{3}{4} = \frac{142}{20} - \frac{15}{20} = \frac{127}{20}$$

b)

$$\frac{6}{5} + 0.4 = \frac{6}{5} + \frac{2}{5} = \frac{8}{5} = 1.6$$

Equation

Example
Write a situation that can be expressed by the equation: $5 \cdot 4 = 20$.

Sample situation: Five students are working together on a project. Each student spends four hours working on his or her portion of the project. The total time spend working on the project is: 5 students $\cdot$ 4 hours for each student = 20 hours.

Division

Example 1
A supermarket advertises a special price of $3.00 for 5 oranges. The regular price is $2.50 for 4 oranges. Compare the unit prices of sale and regular-priced oranges.

To find the unit price of sale and regular-priced oranges, find the price of one orange, or the price per orange. The price of a single orange can be found by dividing the total price by the total number of oranges. The price should be rounded to the nearest cent, or hundredth, since this is the smallest unit of dollars.

Sale price: $\dfrac{\$3.00}{5 \ oranges} = \dfrac{\$0.60}{1 \ orange}$

Regular price $\dfrac{\$2.50}{4 \ oranges} = \dfrac{\$0.63}{1 \ orange}$:

The sale price is: $0.63 – $0.60 = $0.03 less than the regular price.

Example 2
T-shirts are sold in packages of multiple shirts. Three t-shirts are sold in one package for $8.00. Five t-shirts are sold in a second package for $12.00. Compare the price of a single t-shirt from the two packages.

To find the price of each t-shirt, divide the quantity of shirts in each package by the cost of each package. The cost of each shirt should be rounded to the nearest cent, or hundredth, since this is the smallest unit of dollars.

Package 1: $\dfrac{\$8.00}{3} = \$2.67$

Package 2: $\dfrac{\$12.00}{5} = \$2.40$

The price per t-shirt is cheaper if purchasing the five t-shirts for $12.00.

Order of operations

Example
Use the order of operations to evaluate the expression: $14 + 2 \cdot (3 – 1)$.

The first operations to evaluate are any within parenthesis.
$14 + 2 \cdot (3 – 1) = 14 + 2 \cdot 2$
Next, evaluate any multiplication or division.
$14 + 2 \cdot 2 = 14 + 4$
Lastly evaluate any addition or subtraction.
$14 + 4 = 18$

Patterns, Relationships, and Algebraic Reasoning

Ratios to find unknown quantities

Example 1

A recipe for 24 cookies calls for 2 cups of sugar. Find the cups of sugar needed to make 30 cookies.

Using the known quantities, write a ratio relating the cups of sugar to the number of cookies:

$$\frac{2 \ cups}{24 \ cookies}$$

Write a proportion, or equation relating two ratios, and solve for the unknown quantity.

$$\frac{2 \ cups}{24 \ cookies} = \frac{c \ cups}{30 \ cookies}$$
$$60 = 24c$$
$$c = 2\frac{1}{2}$$

Two and a half cups of sugar are needed to make 30 cookies.

Example 2

A map contains a key to relate measurements on the map to real distances. The key on one map says that 2 inches on the map equals 12 miles. Find the distance of a route that is 5 inches long on the map.

Write a proportion that relates the map measurements to real distances. First, write a ratio that relates the information given in the key. The map measurement can be in the numerator, and the real distance in the denominator.

$$\frac{2 \ in}{12 \ mi}$$

Next, write a ratio relating the known map distance to the unknown real distance. The unknown miles can be represented with the letter m.

$$\frac{5 \ in}{m \ mi}$$

A proportion is an equation relating two ratios. Write a proportion and solve it for m.

$$\frac{2 \ in}{12 \ mi} = \frac{5 \ in}{m \ mi}$$
$$2m = 60$$
$$m = 30$$

The route is 30 miles long.

Use of symbols

Example

Students create multiple pieces of artwork and submit them to an art gallery. A batch of artwork arrives, from 4 students. There are a total of 9 pieces of art. Create a drawing to predict the number of pieces of artwork expected from a total of 16 students.

Shapes can be used to represent students and the submitted artwork. Use different shapes to represent students and artwork. Below, squares represent students, and circles represent artwork.

□□□□

There are 16 total students submitting artwork. The original group contained 4 students, so the new group is: $16 \div 4 = 4$ times as large. Draw four sets of the group created showing the relationship between students and artwork.

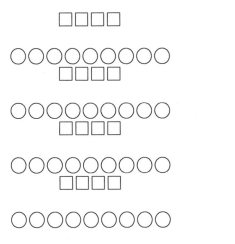

The total pieces of artwork submitted by 16 students is 36.

Tables

Example 1
A kindergarten teacher orders four workbooks for each student. Create a table showing the number of workbooks needed for 1, 2, 3, 4, or 5 students.

The number of workbooks needed increases by four for each additional student. For one student, 4 workbooks are needed.

Number of students	Number of workbooks
1	4
2	4 + 4 = 8
3	8 + 4 = 12
4	12 + 4 = 16
5	16 + 4 = 20

Example 2
Use a table to show the relationship between the perimeters of rectangles with the following dimensions:
Rectangle 1: length: l, width: w
Rectangle 2: length: l, width: $l \cdot 2w$
Rectangle 3: length: l, width: $l \cdot 3w$
Rectangle 4: length: l, width: $l \cdot 4w$
Describe how changing w changed the perimeter of the rectangle.

Create a table showing the dimensions of each rectangle, and the corresponding perimeter.

Length	Width	Perimeter
l	w	$2l + 2w$
l	w	$2l + 4w$
l	w	$2l + 6w$
l	w	$2l + 8w$

As w increased by 1, the perimeter increased by $2w$.

Conversions

Example
One foot is 12 inches. Convert each of the measurements below:
a) 3 feet in inches
b) 20 inches in feet

Write a ratio to show the relationship between feet and inches. If 1 foot = 12 inches, then a ratio to describe the relationship is: $\frac{1\,ft}{12\,in}$. Use the ratio and write proportions to convert each measure. A variable, such as x, can be used to represent the unknown value.

a)
$$\frac{1\,ft}{12\,in} = \frac{3\,ft}{x\,in}$$
$$x = 36$$
3 feet is equal to 36 inches.

b)
$$\frac{1\,ft}{12\,in} = \frac{x\,ft}{20\,in}$$
$$20 = 12x$$
$$x = \frac{20}{12} = \frac{5}{3}$$
20 inches is equal to $\frac{5}{3}$ feet.

Perimeter

Example
Draw a rectangle with width: a and length: b. Describe the perimeter and

write an equation to represent the perimeter of the rectangle.

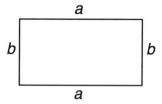

The perimeter of a rectangle is the sum of the length of the sides of the rectangle. The perimeter of the rectangle is: $a + b + a + b$, or $2a + 2b$.

Area

Draw a rectangle width x and length y. Describe the area of the rectangle and write an equation to represent the rectangle's area.

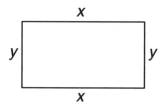

The area of a rectangle is the measurement of the inside of the rectangle. The area of the rectangle is: $x \cdot y$.

Formulating equations

<u>Example</u>
The scale below is balanced. The small blocks each weigh 2 pounds. The large blocks each weigh p pounds.

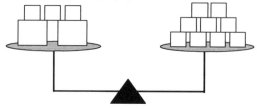

Write an equation showing the relationship between the two sides of the scale.

Given that the two sides of the scale are equal, write an equation relating the blocks on each side of the scale. Represent the weight of each large block with a p, and the weight of each small block is 2 pounds.
$2 + 2 + 2 + p + p = 2 + 2 + 2 + 2 + 2 + 2 + 2 + 2 + 2$
Simplify each side of the equation.
$6 + 2p = 18$

<u>Example 2</u>
A band is hired to perform. The band will be paid $4,000. Tickets to watch the band are sold for $10 each. Write an expression showing the difference between the money earned by selling tickets and the cost of hiring the band.

The cost to hire the band is $4,000. The money earned by selling tickets will depend on the number of tickets sold. Let a variable, such as n, represent the number of tickets sold. The money earned by selling tickets is the money earned for each ticket, $10, times the number of tickets sold, n: $10 \cdot n$. An expression that shows the difference between the money earned by selling tickets and the cost of hiring the band is the money earned minus the band cost: $10 \cdot n - \$4,000$

- 6 -

Geometry and Spatial Reasoning

Acute, obtuse, and right angles

An acute angle is an angle that is less than 90º.

An obtuse angle is an angle that is greater than 90º.

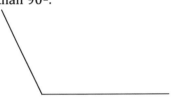

A right angle is an angle that is equal to 90º.

Example
Draw an angle with a measure of 115º. Classify the angle as acute, right, or obtuse.

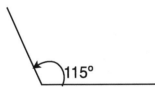

The angle is greater than 90º, and is therefore an obtuse angle.

Angles in triangles and quadrilaterals

The following are relationships involving the angles in triangles and quadrilaterals:
- The sum of the interior angles of a triangle is 180º.
- The smallest angle of a triangle is opposite the shortest side of the triangle. The largest angle of a triangle is opposite the longest side of the triangle.
- The sum of the interior angles of a quadrilateral is 360º.
- Opposite angles of a parallelogram are equivalent.
- A regular quadrilateral is a quadrilateral with four equal sides. The angles of a regular quadrilateral are also equivalent.

Radius and diameter

The radius of a circle is half the length of the diameter. The radius of a circle is any line segment drawn from a point on the circle to the circle's center. The diameter of a circle is a line segment draw from one point on a circle to another that goes through the center of the circle.

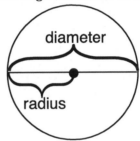

Circumference

The circumference of a circle is $2\pi r$, or πd, where r is the circle's radius and d is the circle's diameter.

Example
Find the circumference of a circle with the given measurements:
a) radius: 120 mm
b) diameter: 8 in

a) circumference = $2\pi(120 \text{ mm}) = 240\pi$ mm
b) circumference = $\pi(8 \text{ in}) = 8\pi$ in

Graphing ordered pairs

Plot the following points on a coordinate plane:
A: (1, 2); B: (5, 3); C: (4, 4)

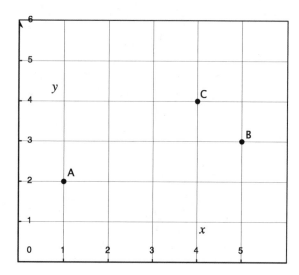

Measurement

Circumference and diameter

<u>Example</u>
Steve bakes a cake in a pan with a 9-inch diameter. He decides to decorate the cake by placing raspberries around its edge. Each raspberry has a diameter of approximately 0.5 inches. Use the circumference of the cake to estimate how many raspberries Steve needs to purchase.

It may be helpful to begin with a diagram. Looking at the top of the Steve's cake, the view would be:

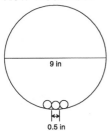

Note that this is not drawn to scale, but is a representation of the problem being solved. To approximate the number of raspberries needed, first find the circumference of the cake. The circumference of a circle is: $2\pi r$, where r is the radius of the circle. To find the radius of the cake, divide the diameter by 2: 9 in ÷ 2 = 4.5 in. The radius of the circle is 4.5 inches. The value pi, π, can be estimated using the fraction: $\frac{22}{7}$, or 3.14. The circumference of the circle is approximately: $2 \cdot \frac{22}{7} \cdot 4.5 = 28.89$. To find the number of raspberries needed, divide the circumference by the approximate diameter of each raspberry: 28.29 ÷ 0.5 = 56.58. Approximately 57 raspberries will be needed to decorate the cake.

Area

<u>Example</u>
Leslie decides to tile her bathroom floor with tiles that are rectangles. Each rectangle has a length of 10 inches and a width of 8 inches. Find the number of tiles needed for a floor with an area of 3600 in².

First, find the area of each tile. The area of a rectangle is: lw, where l is the length of the rectangle, and w is the width. The area of each tile is: 10 in · 8 in = 80 in². To find the number of tiles needed, divide the total area of the floor, 3600 in², by the area of each tile: 3600 in² ÷ 80 in² = 45. Leslie needs 45 tiles.

Temperature

The average temperature on Monday is 51º F. On Tuesday, the average temperature is 8º F lower than the temperature on Monday. On Wednesday, the average temperature is 3º higher than the temperature on Tuesday. Find the temperature on Tuesday and Wednesday.

Use the temperature on Monday, 51º F, to find the temperature on Tuesday. If the average temperature on Tuesday is 8º F less than the temperature on Monday, the temperature on Tuesday is: 51º F – 8º F = 43º F. Use the temperature on Tuesday to find the temperature on Wednesday. If the average temperature on Wednesday is 3º F higher than the temperature on Tuesday, the temperature on Wednesday is: 43º F + 3º F = 46º F.

Volume

<u>Example</u>
A bathtub is approximately shaped like a rectangular prism, with no top. The tub has a length of 60 inches, a width of 24 inches, and a height of 16 inches. The tub is filled halfway with water. Find the volume of the water in the tub.

Drawing a diagram may be helpful. Draw a rectangular prism, with l = 60 inches, w = 24 inches, and h = 16 inches. If the tub is filled halfway, then the height of the water is half of the height of the tub, or 16 inches ÷ 2 = 8 inches. Draw a line representing the fill height of the water.

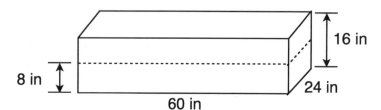

The volume of the water is the volume of the rectangular prism with dimensions: l = 60 in, w = 24 in, and h = 8 in. The volume of a rectangular prism is: lwh = 60 in · 24 in · 8 in = 11,520 in³.

Temperature

The average temperature on Monday is 51º F. On Tuesday, the average temperature is 8º F lower than the temperature on Monday. On Wednesday, the average temperature is 3º higher than the temperature on Tuesday. Find the temperature on Tuesday and Wednesday.

Use the temperature on Monday, 51º F, to find the temperature on Tuesday. If the average temperature on Tuesday is 8º F less than the temperature on Monday, the temperature on Tuesday is: 51º F – 8º F = 43º F. Use the temperature on Tuesday to find the temperature on Wednesday. If the average temperature on Wednesday is 3º F higher than the temperature on Tuesday, the temperature on Wednesday is: 43º F + 3º F = 46º F.

Measuring angles

Example
Draw an angle with a measure of 25º.

There are 100 cm in 1 m. Convert between the measurements below.
a) 1.4 m in cm
b) 218 cm in m

Write a ratio relating the units: $\frac{100 \text{ cm}}{1 \text{ m}}$. Use the ratio to write a proportion to convert the given units.

a) $\frac{100 \text{ cm}}{1 \text{ m}} = \frac{x \text{ cm}}{1.4 \text{ m}}$. Cross multiply to get $x = 140$. Therefore 1.4 m = 140 cm.

b) $\frac{100 \text{ cm}}{1 \text{ m}} = \frac{218 \text{ cm}}{x \text{ m}}$. Cross multiply to get $100x = 218$, or $x = 2.18$. Therefore 218 cm = 2.18 m.

Measurement conversion

Example
There are 12 inches in 1 foot, and 3 feet in 1 yard. Convert between the measurements below.
a) 42 inches to feet
b) 15 feet to yards

Write a ratio relating the inches to feet: $\frac{12 \text{ in}}{1 \text{ ft}}$ and feet to yards: $\frac{3 \text{ ft}}{1 \text{ yd}}$. Use the ratios to write a proportion to convert the given units.

a) $\frac{12 \text{ in}}{1 \text{ ft}} = \frac{42 \text{ in}}{x \text{ ft}}$. Cross multiply to get $12x = 42$, or $x = 3.5$. Therefore 42 inches = 3.5 feet.

b) $\frac{3 \text{ ft}}{1 \text{ yd}} = \frac{15 \text{ ft}}{x \text{ yd}}$. Cross multiply to get $3x = 15$, or $x = 5$. Therefore 15 feet = 5 yards.

Probability and Statistics

Tree diagram

Ted picks his clothing in the morning from a selection of 4 pairs of pants and 3 shirts. Draw a diagram to find the sample space of the selection of an outfit consisting of exactly one pair of pants and one shirt.

A tree diagram can be used to find the number of different ways pants and shirts can be selected. This will show the sample space for the selection of an outfit.

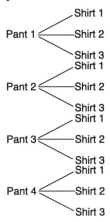

The sample space is the twelve different combinations of pants and shirts.

Graphical representation of data

Example 1
A fast service restaurant offers different types of sandwiches and sides.
Sandwiches: Turkey, Ham, Grilled cheese
Sides: Apple, Potato chips
Write a list of all possible combinations of sandwiches and sides.

Pair each sandwich type with each type of side. It may be helpful to use a table to organize the combinations.

Sandwich	Side
Turkey	Apple
Turkey	Potato chips
Ham	Apple
Ham	Potato chips
Grilled cheese	Apple
Grilled cheese	Potato chips

Example 2
A line plot contains quantitative (numerical) values on a number line, with an *x* or dot above each value for the number of times that value is present in a sample.

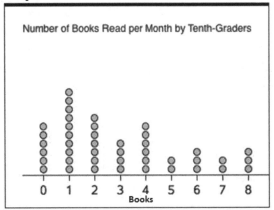

Example 3
A line graph shows the relationship between two quantities. The data points are connected to show the relationship is continuous. The graph below shows the relationship between time, in hours, and distance traveled by car, in miles. The *x*-axis represents time and the *y*-axis represents total distance traveled.

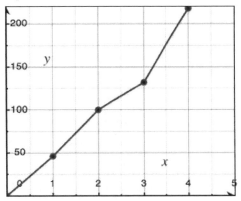

Example 4

A bar graph is a frequency plot. It contains the frequency of discrete data values, which can either be numerical or categorical (such as a dollar amount or category types, such as types of books).

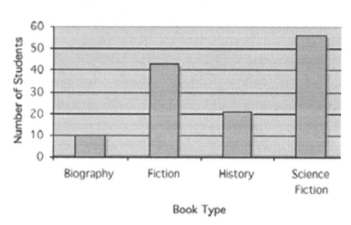

Books Preferred by Tenth-Graders

Example 5

Mr. Glaser records the following grades of students on a 40-point quiz: 18, 27, 29, 30, 34, 35, 35, 37, 40. Represent the data in a stem-and-leaf plot.

The value of the tens place will be the values in the stem, and the value of the ones place will be the values in the leaves. Arrange the values from least to greatest.

Stem	leaf
1	8
2	7 9
3	0 4 5 5 7
4	0

Probability

Example

A six-sided die has sides numbered 1 through 6. Find the probability of rolling a 2.

To find the probability of an event, divide the number of ways the event can occur by the sample space. When rolling a six-

sided die, the sample space is the six possible sides of the die. One of the six sides is a 2. The probability of rolling a 2 is: $P(2) = \frac{\#\ ways\ to\ roll\ a\ 2}{\#\ total\ ways\ to\ roll} = \frac{1}{6}$.

Complement

The complement of an event is all other events in the sample space. The sum of the probability of an event and the probability of all other possible events is 1. Let A represent the event.

P(A) + P(complement of A) = 1

Mean, median, mode, and range

The mean of a data set is the average of the values. It is found by summing the data points and dividing by the total number of points. The median is the middle-most data value. It is found by first arranging the data from least to greatest. If there are an odd number of data points, the median is the middle-most point. If there are an even number of data points, it is the average of the two middle-most points. The mode of a data set is the data value that is repeated the most. The range of a data set is the difference between the greatest data point and least data point.

Example 1
Ten students in Mrs. Mason's class record their ages in months: 163, 179, 165, 180, 158, 180, 179, 174, 180, 165. Find the mean, median, mode, and range of the ages of the students.

The mean is the average age. Sum the ages and divide by 10, the number of ages.

$$\frac{163 + 179 + 165 + 180 + 158 + 180 + 179 + 174 + 180 + 165}{10}$$

$$= \frac{1723}{10} = 172.3$$

The median is the middle-most data point. First sort the ages from least to greatest:
158, 163, 165, 165, 174, 179, 179, 180, 180, 180.
There is an even number of data points, so the median is the average of the two middle-most data points.
$$\frac{174 + 179}{2} = 176.5$$
The mode is the most frequent age, 180 months.
The range is the difference between the greatest and least data points: 180 – 158 = 22 months.

Example 2
A company boasts that its mean starting salary is $61,000. Here is the list of the starting salaries on which the company based its claim.
New Employee Starting Salary
A $27,000;   B $29,000
C $37,000;   D $42,000
E $45,000;   F $49,000
G $55,000;   H $60,000
I $92,000;   J $110,000
K $125,000

Determine what a smart job seeker should inquire about when presented with a mean starting salary figure.
The company presents $61,000 as the mean starting salary, which is entirely accurate but somewhat misleading since more than 70% of the new employees had starting salaries below $61,000. A smart job seeker will inquire about the median starting salary as this is a better indicator of the salary that can be expected, since this will not inflated by salaries that are much larger or lower than the average.

The median salary in this case is $49,000. This is likely to be closer to the starting salary of an average employee.

Circle graph

A circle graph shows the relationship between each item in the collected data set to the whole of data that was collected. The circle graph below represents the percentage of the tenth grade that preferred each of the four types of pets. One hundred percent of responses are included in the circle graph.

Favorite Pet of Tenth-Graders

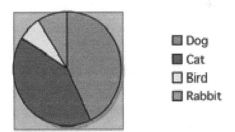

Average

Example
Cara has earned grades of 78, 82, 80, and 94 on her math exams. She has one remaining exam for the term, and the mean of her five exam scores will determine her term average for the math course. Explain what score Cara needs on her fifth exam to earn an 85 average in the course.

Let x represent Cara's score on her fifth exam. To find her term average, sum together the five scores and divide by five.

$$term\ average = \frac{78 + 82 + 80 + 94 + x}{5}$$

If Cara wants to earn an 85 in the course, replace "term average" with 85 and solve for x.

$$85 = \frac{87 + 82 + 80 + 94 + x}{5}$$

$$85 \cdot 5 = 87 + 82 + 80 + 94 + x$$

$$425 = 334 + x$$

$$x = 91$$

For Cara to end the term with an 85 average, she must score a 91 on her fifth exam.

Practice Test #1

Practice Questions

1. Antonio wants to buy a roll of border to finish an art project. At four different shops, he found four different borders he liked. He wants to use the widest of the borders. The list shows the width, in inches, of the borders he found.

$$1\frac{7}{10}, 1.72, 1\frac{3}{4}, 1.695$$

Which roll of border should Antonio buy if he wants to buy the widest border?

  a. $1\frac{7}{10}$
  b. 1.72
  c. $1\frac{3}{4}$
  d. 1.695

2. Daniella wrote a decimal and a fraction which were equivalent to each other. Which pair of numbers could be the pair Daniella wrote?

  a. $0.625, \frac{7}{8}$
  b. $0.375, \frac{3}{8}$
  c. $0.75, \frac{7}{5}$
  d. $0.45, \frac{4}{5}$

3. Glenda poured salt into three salt shakers from a box that contained 26 ounces of salt. She poured 2 ounces of salt into one shaker, 3 ounces of salt into the second shaker, and 4 ounces into the third shaker. She did not pour salt into any other shakers. Which expression best represents the amount of salt left in the box after Glenda poured salt into the three shakers?

  a. $2 - 3 - 4 + 26$
  b. $2 + 3 + 4 - 26$
  c. $26 - 2 + 3 + 4$
  d. $26 - 2 - 3 - 4$

4. Which expression best shows the prime factorization of 750?

  a. $2 \times 3 \times 5^3$
  b. $2 \times 3 \times 5^2$
  c. $2 \times 3 \times 5 \times 25$
  d. $2 \times 3 \times 5^2 \times 25$

5. Place your answer on the provided griddable answer sheet.

Denna has 75 packs of hollyhock seeds, 150 packs of zinnia seeds, and 225 packs of petunia seeds. She wants to make the largest number of gift baskets possible so that each basket has the same number of packs of each kind of flower seed. What is the greatest common factor Denna can use to find the largest number of baskets possible with the same number of packs of each kind of flower seed in each?

6. The drawing shows a window with equal-sized panes. Some of the panes are not tinted, some are tinted a light shade of gray, and some are tinted a very dark shade of gray.

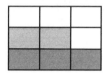

Which number sentence best models the total section of the window that has tinted panes?

a. $\frac{1}{3} + \frac{1}{3} = \frac{2}{3}$

b. $\frac{1}{3} + \frac{2}{9} = \frac{5}{9}$

c. $\frac{1}{9} + \frac{2}{3} = \frac{7}{9}$

d. $\frac{2}{9} + \frac{4}{9} = \frac{2}{3}$

7. Julie shopped for first-aid cream. One large tube held 1.5 fluid ounces and the smallest tube held 0.33 fluid ounces. What is the difference in the number of fluid ounces of cream in the two tubes?

a. 1.8
b. 1.27
c. 1.23
d. 1.17

8. Large boxes of canned beans hold 24 cans of beans and small boxes hold 12 cans. One afternoon, Gerald brought 4 large boxes of canned beans and 6 small boxes of canned beans to the food bank. How many cans of beans did Gerald bring to the food bank that afternoon?

a. 168
b. 192
c. 288
d. 360

9. Jeff saw 25 cars in the school parking lot. If each car brought from 1 to 3 people to school, which is the best estimate of the total number of people arriving to school in the 25 cars?

a. 25
b. 50
c. 75
d. 100

- 16 -

10. Enrique used a formula to find the total cost, in dollars, for repairs he and his helper, Jenny, made to a furnace. The expression below shows the formula he used, with 4 being the number of hours he worked on the furnace and 2 being the number of hours Jenny worked on the furnace. $20 + 35(4 + 2) + 47$

What is the total cost for repairing the furnace?
    a. $189
    b. $269
    c. $277
    d. $377

11. One morning at Jim's café, 25 people ordered juice, 10 ordered milk, and 50 ordered coffee with breakfast. Which ratio best compares the number of people who ordered milk to the number of people who ordered juice?
    a. 5 to 7
    b. 5 to 2
    c. 2 to 7
    d. 2 to 5

12. At the middle school Vanessa attends, there are 240 Grade 6 students, 210 Grade 7 students, and 200 Grade 8 students. Which ratio best compares the number of students in Grade 8 to the number of students in Grade 6 at Vanessa's school?
    a. $5 : 6$
    b. $5 : 11$
    c. $6 : 5$
    d. $7 : 8$

13. The drawing shows a chart used to record completed Math assignments. A checkmark is used to show which assignments are finished.

Math Assignment

Which of the following shows the percentage of Math assignments in the chart which are finished?
    a. 15%
    b. 25%
    c. 55%
    d. 75%

14. A display at the bottom of the laptop computer Erica was using showed that the battery had a 70% charge. Which decimal is equivalent to 70%?
    a. 0.07
    b. 70.0
    c. 7.0
    d. 0.7

15. Harold learned that 6 out of 10 students at his school live within two miles of the school. If 240 students attend Grade 6 at his school, about how many of these students should Harold expect to live within two miles of the school?

    a. 24

    b. 40

    c. 144

    d. 180

16. A unit of liquid measure in the English System of Measure is the gill. The table, shown here, gives conversions from gills to fluid ounces.

Conversion Table

Gills	Fluid Ounces
2	8
4	16
5	20
6	24
10	40

Which equation best describes the relationship between gills, g, and fluid ounces, f?

    a. $f = 8g - 8$

    b. $f = 2g + 4$

    c. $f = 4g$

    d. $4f = g$

17. The table below shows changes in the area of several trapezoids as the lengths of the bases, b_1 and b_2, remain the same and the height, h, changes.

Trapezoids

b_1 (in feet)	b_2 (in feet)	h (in feet)	A (in square feet)
5	7	2	12
5	7	4	24
5	7	6	36
5	7	8	48

Which formula best represents the relationship between A, the areas of these trapezoids, and h, their heights?

    a. $A = 5h$

    b. $A = 6h$

    c. $A = 7h$

    d. $A = 12h$

18. This table shows lengths, widths, and areas of four rectangles. In each rectangle, the length remains 40 meters, but the width changes.

Rectangles

Length	40 meters	40 meters	40 meters	40 meters
Width	20 meters	30 meters	40 meters	50 meters
Perimeter	120 meters	140 meters	160 meters	180 meters

Which formula best represents the relationship between P, the perimeters of these rectangles, and w, their widths?

    a. $P = w + 80$
    b. $P = 2w + 80$
    c. $P = 2(2w + 40)$
    d. $P = 10(w + 40)$

19. A trash company charges a fee of \$80 to haul off a load of trash. There is also a charge of \$0.05 per mile the load must be hauled. Which equation can be used to find c, the cost for hauling a load of trash m miles?

    a. $80(m + 0.05)$
    b. $0.05(m + 80)$
    c. $80m + 0.05$
    d. $0.05m + 80$

20. Thomas drew a polygon with vertices: A, B, C, and D. He measured the angles formed and recorded the information shown here.
$$m\angle A = 70°, m\angle B = 80°, m\angle C = 120°, m\angle D = 90°$$
Which of the angles that Thomas drew is an obtuse angle?

    a. $\angle A$
    b. $\angle B$
    c. $\angle C$
    d. $\angle D$

21. Georgia measured and labeled the angles shown in this drawing.

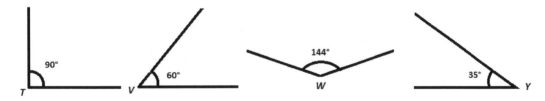

Which of the angles that Georgia measured is a right angle?

    a. $\angle T$
    b. $\angle V$
    c. $\angle W$
    d. $\angle Y$

22. In $\triangle RST$, shown here, $m\angle S$ is 20° less than $m\angle R$.

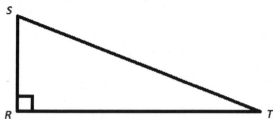

What is the measure of $\angle T$?
    a. 110°
    b. 70°
    c. 50°
    d. 20°

23. Ellen measured $\angle R$ in the parallelogram shown here and found it to be 35°. She knows that $\angle R$ and $\angle T$ have equal measures. She also knows $\angle S$ and $\angle V$ are equal in measure.

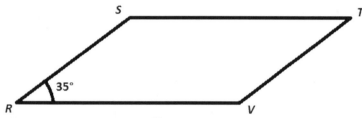

What is the measure of $\angle V$?
    a. 215°
    b. 145°
    c. 70°
    d. 35°

24. A worker put 2 strings of lights around a circular pond in the city park, so that each string of lights went around the entire pond once. The total length of the strings of lights was 100 feet. Which expression, when used by itself, can be used to determine the distance across the center of the pond?
    a. $100 \div \pi$
    b. $\pi \div 100$
    c. $(100 \div 2) \div \pi$
    d. $(\pi \div 100) \div 2$

25. Omar drew a circle on paper by carefully tracing completely around the outside of a CD from a computer game. He measured across the center of the CD and found the distance to be 12 centimeters.

Which expression can be used to find the distance, in centimeters, around the circle Omar made?
    a. $12(\pi)$
    b. $2(12)(\pi)$
    c. $(12 \div 2)(\pi)$
    d. $2(\pi \div 12)$

26. Use this grid to answer the question.

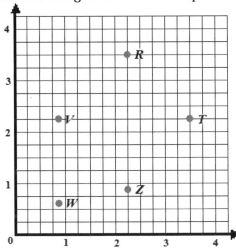

Which ordered pair best represents the coordinates of Point R?
    a. $(2\frac{1}{4}, 3\frac{1}{2})$
    b. $(3\frac{1}{2}, 2\frac{1}{4})$
    c. $(9, 14)$
    d. $(14, 9)$

27. The tires on Ginny's bike are about 20 inches from the top of the tire to the ground. Which of these is closest to the distance around each tire?
    a. 60 inches
    b. 180 inches
    c. 400 inches
    d. 1,200 inches

28. This drawing shows an equilateral triangle and a ruler.

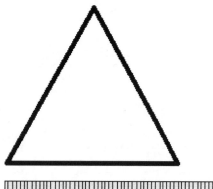

Which is closest to the perimeter of the triangle?
    a. 4.5 centimeters
    b. 9.0 centimeters
    c. 13.5 centimeters
    d. 20.3 centimeters

29. Jessica wrote down the times required for five girls to run a race. The times are shown in this list.

       25.1 seconds, 24.9 seconds, 25.2 seconds, 24.8 seconds, 25.0 seconds

What time is closest to the total for all five runners?
    a. 1 minute and 5 seconds
    b. 1 minute and 25 seconds
    c. 2 minutes and 5 seconds
    d. 2 minutes and 25 seconds

30. The drawing shows a protractor and a trapezoid.

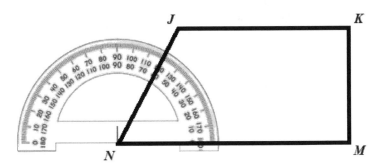

Which is closest to the measure of ∠JNM?
  a. 61°
  b. 79°
  c. 119°
  d. 121°

31. The length of the football field near Gerald's school is 120 yards. What is the length of the field in feet?
  a. 1,440 feet
  b. 360 feet
  c. 400 feet
  d. 12 feet

32. Hillside Middle School students are choosing school colors from three dark colors (black, blue, and brown) and two light colors (white and yellow). Which tree diagram best shows all possible color combinations of one dark color and one light color?

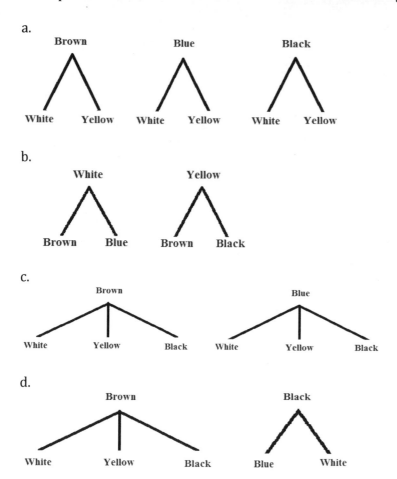

33. Jan played a game which used a fair spinner like the one shown here. Jan needs the arrow to land on green on her next turn.

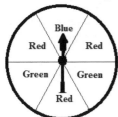

What is the probability that the arrow lands on green when Jan spins one time?

    a. $\frac{1}{6}$

    b. $\frac{1}{3}$

    c. $\frac{1}{2}$

    d. $\frac{2}{3}$

34. Grade 6 students at Fairview Middle School were asked to name their favorite of six school subjects. The plot below shows a summary of their answers. Each X represents 5 students.

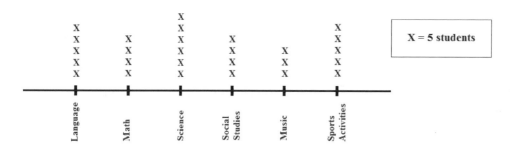

Which graph best represents the data in the plot?

a.

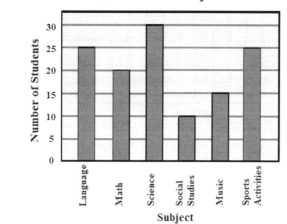

c.

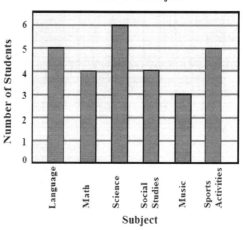

b.

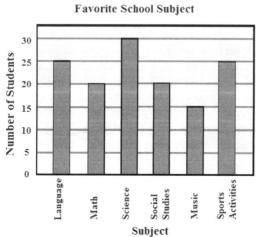

d.

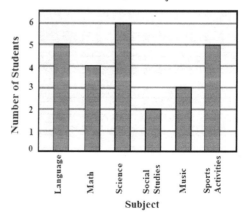

35. Stephen researched the topic of solar-powered lights for his science project. He exposed 10 new solar lights to five hours of sunlight. He recorded the number of minutes each light continued to shine after dark in the list below.

63, 67, 73, 75, 80, 91, 63, 72, 79, 87

Which of these numbers is the mean of the number of minutes in Stephen's list?
    a. 28
    b. 63
    c. 74
    d. 75

36. Sammie had $120 he had earned doing chores for people in his neighborhood. When school started, he spent $50 for shirts, $30 for jeans, and $40 for school supplies. Which graph best represents how Sammy spent his $120?

a.

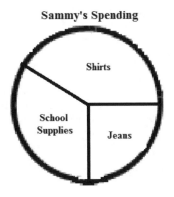

c.

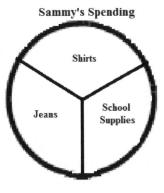

b.

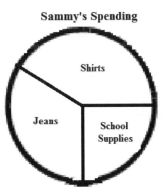

d.

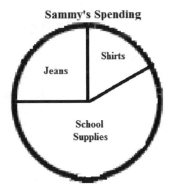

37. Anna and other members of her club sold caps to commemorate their city's 100th birthday. The caps sold for $14 and came in four colors. The club made $3,360 in total sales from selling the caps. The graph below shows the part of the total sales that each color represented.

Colors of Caps Sold

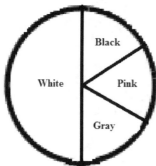

Which number is closest to the combined number of white and pink caps sold by Anna's club members?
    a. 40
    b. 80
    c. 120
    d. 160

38. James and his driving partner, Larissa, recently drove a truck from Dallas, TX to Los Angeles, CA. The total distance they drove was 1,380 miles. James is paid $0.35 per mile he drives and Larissa is paid $0.30 per mile she drives. What additional information is needed to find the amount James should be paid for the trip?
    a. The total number of hours each person drove
    b. The total number of miles each person drove
    c. The total amount of fuel the truck used
    d. The total weight of the truck and cargo

39. Petra installed 10 light fixtures at a new warehouse that was being built. Each of the fixtures required 3 light bulbs. The bulbs come in packages of 5 and cost $8 per package. What was the total cost for the bulbs required for all of the fixtures Petra installed at the warehouse?
    a. $16
    b. $48
    c. $120
    d. $240

40. Some wind generators have blades that look like propellers. When the wind blows, these blades turn in a circle and make electricity. One type has blades that are 100 feet long. If the blades on this type of wind generator turn 15 times each minute, what would be a reasonable distance for the blade tip to travel in 1 minute?
    a. 1,500 feet
    b. 3,000 feet
    c. 4,500 feet
    d. 9,000 feet

41. Tomas needs $100 to buy a telescope he wants. He received $40 as a gift and spent $10 on a book about telescopes. He earned $35 doing small jobs for his family. The steps Tomas can use to find the amount he still needs to save to buy the telescope are shown here in incorrect order.

Step R: Subtract 65 from 100.
Step S: Subtract 10 from 40.
Step T: Add 35 to 30.

Which sequence shows the steps in the correct order?

a. T, S, R
b. T, R, S
c. S, T, R
d. R, S, T

42. *Place your answer on the provided griddable answer sheet.*

Kerianne collected the weights of her friends. What is the range of her friends' weight?

55 lbs, 63 lbs, 48 lbs, 72 lbs, 61 lbs, 68 lbs

43. The repeating pattern shown below uses the same four figures over and over again.

Fig. 1   **Fig. 2**   **Fig. 3**   **Fig. 4**   **Fig. 5**   **Fig. 6** ...

Which of the four figures will the figure in the 31st position look like?

a. Figure 1
b. Figure 2
c. Figure 3
d. Figure 4

44. Jason wants to put dry fertilizer on the grass in his front yard. The yard is 20 feet wide and 45 feet long. Each pound of the fertilizer he plans to use is enough for 150 square feet. Which procedure could Jason use to determine the correct amount of fertilizer to use on the entire yard?

a. Divide 150 by 20 and divide 150 by 45, and then add those quotients together
b. Add 20 and 45, double that total, and then divide that total by 150
c. Multiply 20 by 45, and then subtract 150 from that product
d. Multiply 20 by 45, and then divide that product by 150

45. Two sets of numbers are shown here. In each set, the terms increase by the same amount each time.

Set M = {1, 4, 7, 10, 13, ...}
Set V = {1, 3, 5, 7, 9, ...}

What is the first number greater than 20 which is a member of both Set M and Set V?

a. 21
b. 23
c. 25
d. 27

- 29 -

46. Antoinette had $50 she had saved. At a craft show, she bought 2 pairs of earrings for $10 each and a picture for $12. She also spent $7 on lunch. If she spent no other money, how much money should Antoinette have left from the $50?
    a. $35, because 50 – (10 +12) + 7 = 35
    b. $25, because 50 – [2(10) +12] + 7 = 25
    c. $21, because 50 – (10 + 12 + 7) = 21
    d. $11, because 50 – [2(10) + 12 +7] = 11

47. *Place your answer on the provided griddable answer sheet.*
Find the least common multiple for the following numbers:
            8 and 6

48. Candace's shoelace broke. She measured the unbroken shoelace and finds that she needs a replacement lace that is at least 16 inches long. The store has the following lengths available. $15\frac{7}{10}$, 16.25 , $\frac{47}{3}$, 15.5
Which one of the following lace lengths would be long enough to replace the broken shoelace?
    a. $15\frac{7}{10}$
    b. 16.25
    c. $\frac{47}{3}$
    d. 15.5

49. Nadia is working summer jobs. She earns $5 for every dog she walks, $2 for bringing back a trashcan, $1 for checking the mail, and $5 for watering the flowers. Nadia walks 3 dogs, brings back 5 trashcans, checks the mail for 10 neighbors, and waters the flowers at 6 houses. Which expression can be used to find out how much money Nadia earned?
    a. $2(5) +$6(10) + $1
    b. $10(6) + $1 + $5
    c. $5(3+6) + $2(5) + $1(10)
    d. $15 + $10 + $16

50. Only 8% of the dogs were solid white. Which decimal is equivalent to 8%?
    a. 0.08
    b. 80.0
    c. 8.0
    d. 0.8

51. Use this grid to answer the question.

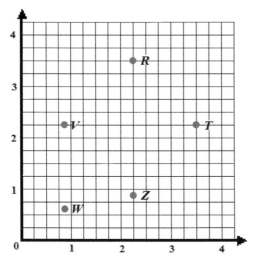

Which of the points on the grid best represents the point at $(2\frac{1}{4}, \frac{7}{8})$?

 a. T
 b. V
 c. W
 d. Z

52. Place your answer on the provided griddable answer sheet.
The recipe called for 2 pints of milk. How many cups of milk are needed?

Answers and Explanations

TEKS Standard §111.26(b)(2)(D)

1. C: To answer this question correctly, convert all numbers to decimal form to make them easy to compare. Since two of the numbers are already in decimal form, we only need to convert $1\frac{7}{10}$ and $1\frac{3}{4}$ to decimal form.

$$7 \div 10 = 0.7, \text{ so } 1\frac{7}{10} = 1.7$$
$$\text{and } 3 \div 4 = 0.75, \text{ so } 1\frac{3}{4} = 1.75$$

Therefore, by comparing place values from left to right of 1.7, 1.72, 1.75 and 1.695, we see that 1.695 is least, 1.7 is next greatest, 1.72 is next, and 1.75 is greatest. So, Antonio should buy the border that is $1\frac{3}{4}$ inches wide.

TEKS Standard §111.26(b)(4)(G)

2. B: To answer this question, one method that can be used is to convert all the fractions to decimal form so it is easier to compare them to each other. This can be done by simply dividing, since the fraction sign means division.

$$7 \div 8 = 0.875$$
$$3 \div 8 = 0.375$$
$$7 \div 5 = 1.4$$
$$4 \div 5 = 0.8$$

So, the only pair of numbers in which the fraction is equivalent to the decimal is in answer B.

TEKS Standard §111.26(b)(3)(D)

3. D: Only answer D correctly shows each amount of salt being subtracted from the original total amount of 26 ounces that was in the box.

TEKS Standard §111.26(b)(7)(A)

4. A: There is more than one way to solve this problem. One method is to use the fact that the number ends in 0. This means 10 is a factor. So, 10 × 75 = 750. The factor 10 has prime factors of 2 and 5. The factor 75 has factors of 3 and 25 and the 25 has two factors of 5. Putting the prime factors in order, least to greatest, and showing the three factors of 5 with an exponent of 3 gives us answer A: $2 \times 3 \times 5^3$.

TEKS Standard §111.26(b)(2)

5. The correct answer is 75. There is more than one way to solve this problem. One method is to find the greatest common factor of 75, 150, and 225. Find the prime factors for each number.

75 = 3 × 5 × 5
150 = 2 × 3 × 5 × 5
225 = 3 × 3 × 5 × 5

Notice that the common factors of all three numbers is 3, 5, and 5. Multiply 3 × 5 × 5 to get 75, the greatest common factor. So, she can make 75 baskets that have the same number of each kind of seed.

TEKS Standard §111.26(b)(3)

6. B: To answer this question, that there are 9 equal-sized panes in the window. Of the 9 panes, 3 have a dark tint and can be represented by the fraction, $\frac{3}{9}$, which is equivalent to $\frac{1}{3}$. 2 of the panes are lightly tinted and can be represented by $\frac{2}{9}$. So, the number sentence, $\frac{1}{3} + \frac{2}{9} = \frac{5}{9}$ best represents the total section of the window which is tinted.

TEKS Standard §111.26(b)(3)

7. D: To find the difference, subtract. It is important to align decimal places. Note, when subtracting here, the digit in the hundredths place in 0.33 has no digit aligned above it. We must add a zero to 1.5 so that we can align the hundredths places correctly. Now we can subtract 33 hundredths from the 50 hundredths to get 17 hundredths. So, we get 1.17 as our correct answer.

TEKS Standard §111.26(b)(3)(D)

8. A: Multiply 24 by 4 to get 96 and multiply 12 by 6 to get 72. Then, add 96 and 72 to get the correct answer, 168.

TEKS Standard §111.26(b)(2)

9. B: If each car brought from 1 to 3 people, then 50 is the best estimate of the number of people that could have arrived in the 25 cars. 25 is too low because this would mean only 1 person could have arrived in each car. 75 and 100 are too high, because then this would mean 3 or more people arrived in each car. The answer, 50 people, would mean that each car brought 2 people each, which is the average number of people who arrived per car.

TEKS Standard §111.26(b)(3)

10. C: To solve this formula, follow the order of operations. First, add what is in the parenthesis, 4 + 2, to get 6. Then, multiply the 6 by 35 to get 210. Last, we should add 20 + 210 + 47 to get 277.

TEKS Standard §111.26(b)(5)

11. D: Note that the ratio asked for is the number of people who ordered milk to the number who ordered juice. The number of people who ordered coffee does not matter here. This compares 10 to 25, and the order is important here. Since the ratio is with the number of people who ordered milk first, the 10 must come first. So, the ratio is 10 to 25, but the ratio can be written in simpler form by dividing both numbers in the ratio by 5, to get the ratio: 2 to 5.

TEKS Standard §111.26(b)(5)

12. A: One way to answer this question is to name the ratio: 200 to 240, then write the ratio in simplest terms by dividing both terms by the greatest common factor, 40, to get 5 to 6. It should be noted that the number of Grade 7 students is not important for this problem. Also, the order of the ratio matters. Since it asks for the ratio using the number of Grade 8 students first, the ratio is 200 to 240 and not the other way around.

TEKS Standard §111.26(b)(5)

13. D: There are 15 of the 20 assignments with check marks indicating a finished assignment. Since the fraction $\frac{1}{20}$ represents 5%, then 15 times 5% gives 75% of the assignments finished.

TEKS Standard §111.26(b)(4)(G)

14. D: To correctly write a percent as a decimal, the percent sign is dropped and the number is rewritten with the decimal point two places to the left. This is because a percent is always a value out of 100 and the second place after the decimal point is the hundredths place. So, 70% = 0.70 and the zero at the end after the decimal can be dropped.

TEKS Standard §111.26(b)(3) and (4)(C)

15. C: One way to find this answer is to set up a proportion: $\frac{6}{10} = \frac{G}{240}$, in which G represents the number of Grade 6 students living within two miles of the school. To solve the proportion, we should cross-multiply. So, 10 times G = 6 times 240. This gives the equation: $10G = 1,440$. To solve the equation we divide both sides of the equation by 10, which gives G = 144.

TEKS Standard §111.26(b)(5)(A)

16. C: Looking at the chart, a pattern can be seen in the relationship between the number of gills and the number of fluid ounces. Each number of gills in the first column, when multiplied by 4, gives the number of fluid ounces in the second column. So, f equals 4 times g, or $f = 4g$.

TEKS Standard §111.26(b)(8)(C)

17. B: The formula for the area of trapezoids is not necessarily needed here to do this problem. Since the relationship between the area, A, and the height, h, can be seen in the chart, looking at the third and fourth columns to see if there is a pattern will show a relationship between the variables. Each value in the area column is equal to 6 times the value in the height column. So, we get $A = 6h$.

TEKS Standard §111.26(b)(8)(C)

18. B: To answer this question, start with the perimeter formula, $P = 2(l + w)$ and substitute values that are known to remain the same. So, $P = 2(l + w)$ becomes $P = 2(40 + w)$. Then we distribute, multiplying both numbers inside the parenthesis by 2 and get $P = 80 + 2w$. Writing the variable first in the expression gives us: $P = 2w + 80$.

TEKS Standard §111.26(b)(6)(C)

19. D: The amount charged for miles hauled will require us to multiply the number of miles by $0.05. The charge for each load of $80 is not changed by the number of miles hauled. That will be added to the amount charged for miles hauled. So, the equation needs to show 0.05 times miles plus 80, or $c = 0.05m + 80$.

TEKS Standard §111.26(b)(8)

20. C: An obtuse angle measures between 90 and 180 degrees and $\angle C$ is the only choice which measured in that range.

TEKS Standard §111.26(b)(8)

21. A: A right angle, by definition, measures 90 degrees and $\angle T$ is the only choice which has a measure of 90°.

TEKS Standard §111.26(b)(8)(A)

22. D: The box symbol shown at $\angle R$ means that $\angle R$ measures 90°. Since we are told $m\angle S$ is 20° less than $m\angle R$, subtract 90 – 20 to get 70. This means that $m\angle S = 70°$. The sum of $m\angle R$ and $m\angle S$ is found by adding: $90 + 70 = 160$. The sum of all angles in a triangle always adds up to 180°, so subtracting 180 – 160 results in a difference of 20. So, $m\angle T$ is 20°.

TEKS Standard §111.26(b)(8)

23. B: The angles opposite each other in a parallelogram are equal in measure. So, $\angle R$ has an equal measure to $\angle T$, or 35°. The sum of the measures of these two angles is $35 + 35 = 70$. The sum of the measures of all four angles of a quadrilateral is 360°. We subtract 360 – 70 to get 290. So, 290° is the sum of the measures of the other two equal angles, $\angle S$ and $\angle V$. Then we divide 290 by 2 to get 145. We know that $\angle V$ has a measure of 145°.

TEKS Standard §111.26(b)(8)

24. C: To find the diameter (distance across a circle at the center), the circumference (the distance around the outside of a circle) can be divided by π. However, since the worker put 2 strings of lights around the pond, and a circumference is just the perimeter going around the pond once, we must first divide by 2. So, $100 \div 2$ gives us the circumference, which we then divide by π, giving the expression: $(100 \div 2) \div \pi$.

TEKS Standard §111.26(b)(8)

25. A: The distance across the center of the circle, 12 centimeters, is the diameter of the circle. The distance around the circle, drawn by Omar, is the circumference of that circle. The formula for finding the circumference of a circle is: $C = \pi d$. The expression that can be used substitutes the 12 for d and we get 12π.

TEKS Standard §111.26(b)(11)

26. A: Each of the units represents $\frac{1}{4}$ since there are 4 spaces between each unit. The point R is 9 units right of the $y-$axis, or $\frac{9}{4}$, which is equivalent to $2\frac{1}{4}$, and 14 units up from the $x-$axis, or $\frac{14}{4}$, which is equivalent to $3\frac{1}{2}$. An ordered pair always has the $x-$coordinate (how much to the right or left the point is) first, and then the $y-$coordinate (how much up or down the point is). This is why Answer B is incorrect. So, the correct answer is $\left(2\frac{1}{4}, 3\frac{1}{2}\right)$.

TEKS Standard §111.26(b)(8)
27. A: The distance from the top of the tire to the ground that is given is the diameter of the tire. The distance around the tire is the circumference. To find the circumference, multiply the diameter, 20, by π. Since 3 is fairly close to the value of π, 20 times 3 gives 60 inches.

TEKS Standard §111.26(b)(8)
28. C: The ruler is used to determine the length of one side of the triangle, which is about 4.5 centimeters. Since this is an equilateral triangle, all three sides are of equal length. To find the perimeter, we add up all of the sides. However, since they are all the same length, we can just multiply 4.5 centimeters by 3 to get 13.5 centimeters.

TEKS Standard §111.26(b)(3)
29. C: A close estimate for the total time for all five runners is 125 seconds, which is found by adding 25.1 + 24.9 + 25.2 + 24.8 + 25.0. Then, to convert seconds to minutes, divide by 60 seconds (since there are 60 seconds in a minute) to get 2 with remainder of 5, or 2 minutes and 5 seconds.

TEKS Standard §111.26(b)(8)
30. A: Since segment NM lies along the right side of the protractor, we read the inside scale. The segment NM passes between 60° and 70°, much closer to the 60°, so the correct answer is 61°.

TEKS Standard §111.26(b)(4)(H)
31. B: There are 3 feet in every yard. Since we are converting from a larger unit to a smaller unit, we should multiply the number of the larger unit by the conversion factor. That is 120 times 3 equals 360.

TEKS Standard §111.26(b)(1)(D)
32. A: Only this tree diagram shows all possible color combinations of one dark color and one light color, where the two options of a light color are shown for each of the three possible dark color options. So, there will be six possibilities altogether.

TEKS Standard §111.26(b)(5)
33. B: There are 2 green sections on the spinner and the spinner has 6 sections in all. The probability of spinning green is 2 out of 6, when expressed as a fraction is $\frac{2}{6}$. Written in simplest terms, the fraction is $\frac{1}{3}$.

TEKS Standard §111.26(b)(12)(A)
34. B: Notice that the vertical scale should be 0 to 30 by 5's since each of the X's in the plot represent 5 students. Also, each column should represent a number from the line plot. For example, since Language and Sports Activities both show 5 X's, and each X represents 5 students, 5 times 5 = 25. The subjects of Math and Social Studies both show 4 X's, so 4 times 5 = 20. All of the values are found in this way and the only chart that shows these values is B.

TEKS Standard §111.26(b)(12)(C)
35. D: The mean is just the average. To calculate this, find the total of all 10 numbers by adding. Then, divide that total by 10 because that is the number of data points. The total is 750, so the mean of this group of numbers is 75.

TEKS Standard §111.26(b)(12)(A)

36. A: The appropriate fractions can be found by putting the amount of money spent on each category over the total amount of money spent.

$\frac{50}{120}$ is a little less than half, since half of 120 is 60. $\frac{30}{120}$ simplifies to $\frac{1}{4}$ and $\frac{40}{120}$ simplifies to $\frac{1}{3}$. This means that Sammy spent almost $\frac{1}{2}$ his money on shirts, $\frac{1}{4}$ of his money on jeans, and $\frac{1}{3}$ of his money on school supplies. The graph in A best represents those fractions.

TEKS Standard §111.26(b)(13)(A)

37. D: To answer this question, the total number of caps sold must be found by dividing the total sales, 3,360, by the price of each cap, 14. 3,360 ÷ 14 = 240, so 240 caps were sold in total. So, looking at the graph, it appears that about half of the caps were white, around 120. The graph also shows that the other 3 colors were sold in about equal numbers, so dividing the other half, 120, by 3, gives around 40. Then, adding 120 white caps and 40 pink caps, gives an answer of 160. The club had close to 160 combined sales of white and pink caps.

TEKS Standard §111.26(b)(9)

38. B: Since each person is paid by the number of miles driven, one must know not the total miles for the trip, but the miles each person drove. The fuel, weight, or hours do not matter for this problem.

TEKS Standard §111.26(b)(3)

39. B: To answer this question, find the total number of bulbs required by multiplying 10 by 3. The number of packages of bulbs required can be found by dividing this total number of bulbs, 30, by 5, to find that 6 packages are needed. Then, multiplying 6 by the cost per package, 8, we find that the total cost for all the bulbs needed was $48.

TEKS Standard §111.26(b)(8)

40. D: To find this answer, first estimate the distance the tip of the blade travels in one spin. To do this, we must first realize that the length of the blade is the radius of the circle. The distance the tip of the blade travels is the circumference of the circle. Using the formula, $C = 2\pi r$, we multiply the length of the blade by 2π (a reasonable estimate for π is about 3), so 2 times 100 times 3 is 600. This circumference is the distance traveled in one spin. Since the blade turns 15 times in one minute, we can multiply 600 by 15. We find that the tip of the blade travels about 9,000 feet in one minute.

TEKS Standard §111.26(b)(1)(B)

41. C: The first step would be to subtract the $10 he spent on the book from the gift, $40. This gives us $30. This is how much Tomas still has. We add the $35 he earned to the $30 remaining from the gift, which gives $65, the amount Tomas has in total. Then we subtract $65 from the $100 cost of the telescope to find the amount Tomas still needs to save.

TEKS Standard §111.26(b)(12)(C)

42. The correct answer is 24. Begin by arranging the different weights from least to greatest:
48 lbs, 55 lbs, 61 lbs, 63 lbs 68 lbs, 72 lbs. Range is the difference between the highest and lowest values in a set of data; therefore, 72 – 48 = 24.

TEKS Standard §111.26(b)(1)(B)

43. C: Since the pattern repeats the same 4 figures, each multiple of 4 looks like Fig. 4 (4, 8, 12, ... , 28, 32, ...). The figure in the 31st position is one less than 32, so it should look like the figure left of Fig. 4. That figure is Fig. 3.

TEKS Standard §111.26(b)(1)(B) and (3)

44. D: This procedure first finds the area to be fertilized, by multiplying the length and width of the rectangular yard. Then, it divides that area by the area each pound of fertilizer will cover.

TEKS Standard §111.26(b)(2)

45. C: Notice that Set M starts with 1 and increases by adding 3 each time, so the numbers more than 20 in this set are: (22, 25, 28, 31, ...) Set V is the set of odd numbers, so the numbers in this set greater than 20 are: (21, 23, 25, 27, 29, ...) The first number common to both sets is 25.

TEKS Standard §111.26(b)(3)

46. D: Antoinette bought 2 pairs of earrings at $10 each. To find the amount of money spent on the earrings, 10 must be multiplied by 2. Then adding that $20 to the $12 she paid for the picture and also adding $7 for lunch, she spent $39 in all. $50 – $39 = $11

TEKS Standard §111.26(b)(2)

47. The least common multiple of two numbers is the smallest, none zero, multiple that is common to both numbers.
Multiples of 8 are: 0, 8, 16, 24
Multiples of 6 are: 0, 6, 12, 18, 24
Therefore the least common multiple is 24.

TEKS Standard §111.26(b)(2)

48. C: It is easier to think as the required 16 inches as 16.00 and convert all answer choices to a decimal to compare. Anything greater than 16.00 would be sufficient.
$15\frac{7}{10}$ is equal to 15.7, $\frac{47}{3}$ is equivalent to 15.67 and 15.5 remains 15.5. These three choices are all slightly less than the required 16.00 inches; therefore making 16.25 inches the only adequate choice.

TEKS Standard §111.26(b)(3) and (9)

49. C: Since she earns $5 for walking dogs and watering flowers, this term can be combined to simplify the equation. The other terms for bringing back trashcans and checking the mail are straight multiplication.

TEKS Standard §111.26(b)(5)(C)

50. A: To correctly write a percent as a decimal, the percent sign is dropped and the number is rewritten with the decimal point two places to the left. If there is not two digits in the percent, a zero is used as a place holder. This is because a percent is always a value out of 100 and the second place after the decimal point is the hundredths place. So, 8% = 0.08.

TEKS Standard §111.26(b)(11)

51. D: Each of the units represents $\frac{1}{4}$. The point Z is 9 units right of the $y-$ axis or $\frac{9}{4}$ units, which is equivalent to $2\frac{1}{4}$. The point R is also 9 units from the $y-$ axis, or $\frac{9}{4}$, which is equivalent to $2\frac{1}{4}$. Be careful to notice that coordinate pairs always come in the order of the $x-$ coordinate and then the $y-$ coordinate, and is defined by the pair of numbers. The $y-$ coordinate for Z is $\frac{7}{8}$, while Point R has a $y-$ coordinate of $3\frac{1}{2}$.

TEKS Standard §111.26(b)(4)(H)

52. The correct answer is 4. Each pint is equivalent to 2 cups; therefore 2 pints is equivalent to 4 cups.

Practice Test #2

Practice Questions

1. Four students measured the length of the pencil each was using. The list shows the lengths, in centimeters, of the four pencils.

   17.03 cm, 17.4 cm, 17.31 cm, 17.09 cm

Which list shows the lengths of the pencils in order, from shortest to longest?
   a. 17.4 cm, 17.31 cm, 17.09 cm, 17.03 cm
   b. 17.03 cm, 17.09 cm, 17.4 cm, 17.31 cm
   c. 17.4 cm, 17.03 cm, 17.09 cm, 17.31 cm
   d. 17.03 cm, 17.09 cm, 17.31 cm, 17.4 cm

2. Castor collects only baseball and football cards. He has 40 baseball cards and 10 football cards. Which decimal best shows the part of his entire card collection represented by his baseball cards?
   a. 0.8
   b. 0.75
   c. 0.4
   d. 0.25

3. Which expression best shows the prime factorization of 630?
   a. $2 \times 3 \times 105$
   b. $2 \times 5 \times 7 \times 9$
   c. $2 \times 3^2 \times 5 \times 7$
   d. $2^2 \times 3^2 \times 5 \times 7$

4. Place your answer on the provided griddable sheet.
At LBJ Middle School, there are 240 Sixth Grade students, 180 Seventh Grade students, and 150 Eighth Grade students. The principal wants to make groups with students from each grade in every group. She wants as many groups as possible with equal numbers of students from each grade in each group. What is the greatest common factor the principal can use to find the largest number of groups possible with the same number of students from each grade?

5. A club is making necklaces in school colors. They plan to use an equal number of blue beads and silver beads on each necklace. The blue beads come in bags of 60 and the silver beads come in bags of 80. What is the smallest number of bags of each color the club can purchase to have an equal number of each color bead with no beads left when the necklaces are finished?
   a. 3 bags of blue and 4 bags of silver
   b. 4 bags of blue and 3 bags of silver
   c. 40 bags of blue and 30 bags of silver
   d. 80 bags of blue and 60 bags of silver

- 40 -

6. Olga drew the regular figure shown here. She painted part of the figure a light color and part of it a darker color. She left the rest of the figure white.

Which of the following equations best models the part of the figure Olga left white?

a. $1 - \frac{1}{3} - \frac{1}{3} = \frac{1}{3}$

b. $1 - \frac{1}{6} - \frac{1}{6} = \frac{2}{3}$

c. $1 - \frac{1}{6} - \frac{1}{2} = \frac{1}{3}$

d. $1 - \frac{1}{2} - \frac{1}{3} = \frac{2}{3}$

7. Evan measured the amount of rain in the gauge over the weekend. On Saturday, he measured $1\frac{6}{10}$ inches and on Sunday, $\frac{8}{10}$ inches. What is the total amount of rain, in inches, Evan measured on those two days, written in the simplest form?

a. $1\frac{14}{20}$

b. $1\frac{4}{10}$

c. $1\frac{2}{5}$

d. $2\frac{2}{5}$

8. Rafael purchased 8 new tires for the two family cars. The price of each tire was $144, including taxes. He agreed to make 18 equal monthly payments, interest-free, to pay for the tires. What will be the amount Rafael should pay each month?
   a. $16
   b. $32
   c. $64
   d. $128

9. A farmer had about 150 bags of potatoes on his trailer. Each bag contained from 23 to 27 pounds of potatoes. Which is the best estimate of the total number of pounds of potatoes on the farmer's trailer?
   a. 3,000
   b. 3,700
   c. 4,100
   d. 5,000

10. William needs to find the value of the expression below. What is the value of this expression?   40 − 4(3 − 1)
    a. 29
    b. 32
    c. 72
    d. 107

11. Elena counted the number of birds that came to her bird bath one afternoon. While she watched, 20 sparrows, 16 finches, 4 wrens, and 10 jays came to the bird bath. Which ratio, in simplest form, compares the number of finches that Elena counted to the number of sparrows?
    a. 4 : 5
    b. 4 : 9
    c. 16 : 20
    d. 20 : 36

12. One cold afternoon at a small café, 20 people drank hot tea, 45 drank coffee, and 15 drank hot chocolate. Which ratio compares the number of people who drank coffee to the number who drank tea?
    a. 4 to 13
    b. 4 to 9
    c. 9 to 4
    d. 3 to 1

13. A lake near Armando's home is reported to be 80% full of water. Which fraction is equivalent to 80% and in simplest form?
    a. $\dfrac{1}{80}$

    b. $\dfrac{8}{10}$

    c. $\dfrac{4}{5}$

    d. $\dfrac{80}{1}$

14. The rectangle in this drawing is divided into equal-sized parts, with some of them shaded a darker color.

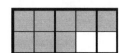

What percent best represents the part of the rectangle that is shaded a darker color?
    a. 8%
    b. 20%
    c. 53%
    d. 80%

15. Annette read that out of 20 televisions sold in her state last year, 3 were Brand V. If a furniture store near her home sold 360 televisions last year, about how many should Annette expect to be Brand V?

    a. 18
    b. 54
    c. 1,080
    d. 2,400

16. The table below gives the positions of several terms in a sequence and the values of those terms.

Sequence

Position of term, n	Value of Term
1	1
2	6
3	11
4	16
5	21
n	?

Which rule can be used to find the value of n?

    a. 5n
    b. 6n
    c. 5n − 4
    d. 6n − 5

17. Julia has a cell phone contract with a monthly charge of $45. She bought a phone with a one-time price of $50 with that contract. Which table best represents the total of all charges which should be paid at the end of each month of the contract?

a.

Number of Months	1	2	3	4	5	6
Total Charges	$45	$90	$135	$180	$225	$270

b.

Number of Months	1	2	3	4	5	6
Total Charges	$95	$140	$185	$230	$275	$320

c.

Number of Months	1	2	3	4	5	6
Total Charges	$95	$190	$285	$380	$475	$570

d.

Number of Months	1	2	3	4	5	6
Total Charges	$50	$95	$140	$185	$230	$275

18. This table shows bases, heights, and areas of four triangles. In each triangle, the base remains the same and the height changes.

Triangles

Base, b	30 yards	30 yards	30 yards	30 yards
Height, h	20 yards	40 yards	60 yards	80 yards
Area, A	300 square yards	600 square yards	900 square yards	1200 square yards

Which formula best represents the relationship between A, the areas of these triangles, and h, their heights?

a. $A = \dfrac{h}{30}$

b. $A = \dfrac{h}{15}$

c. $A = 30h$

d. $A = 15h$

19. An automobile mechanic charges \$65 per hour when repairing an automobile. There is also a charge for the parts required. Which equation can the mechanic use to calculate the charge, c, to repair an automobile which requires h hours and p dollars worth of parts?

a. $c = 65(h + p)$
b. $c = 65h + p$
c. $c = 65p + h$
d. $c = h + p$

20. Gloria created a shape with vertices: N, P, R, and S. She measured the angles formed at the vertices and wrote the information shown here.

$$m\angle N = 90°, m\angle P = 70°, m\angle R = 100°, m\angle S = 100°$$

Which of the angles Gloria created is an acute angle?

a. $\angle N$
b. $\angle P$
c. $\angle R$
d. $\angle S$

21. Robert drew the angles shown here. He measured and labeled them.

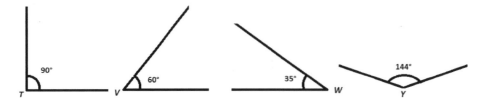

Which of the angles is an obtuse angle?

a. $\angle T$
b. $\angle V$
c. $\angle W$
d. $\angle Y$

- 44 -

22. Greg knows that in the triangle below, $m\angle X$ is 50° more than $m\angle V$.

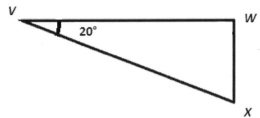

What is the measure of $\angle W$?
    a. 20°
    b. 50°
    c. 70°
    d. 90°

23. Silvia knows that in this shape,
$\angle M$ is equal in measure to $\angle K$, and that the measure of $\angle N$ is 4 times the measure of $\angle K$.

What is the measure of $\angle L$?
    a. 36°
    b. 72°
    c. 144°
    d. 288°

24. Jeremy put a heavy chalk mark on the tire of his bicycle. His bike tire is 27 inches from the ground across the center to the top of the tire. When he rolled the bike, the chalk left marks on the sidewalk. Which expression can be used to best determine the distance, in inches, the bike rolled from the first mark to the fourth mark?
    a. $3(27\pi)$
    b. $4\pi(27)$
    c. $(27 \div 3)\pi$
    d. $(27 \div 4)\pi$

25. Lucinda created a game which requires a circle with a line segment 16 meters long from the circle to the center of the circle as shown here. She wants to paint the required circle and the segment on the parking lot.

16 meters

Which expression can be used by itself to determine the completed length of the circle and segment Lucinda will need to paint?

    a. 16π

    b. $2(16\pi)$

    c. $16\pi + 16$

    d. $2(16\pi) + 16$

26. There are five points labeled on this grid.

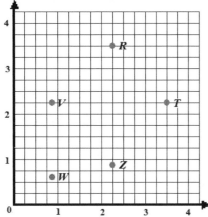

Which of the points on the grid best represents the point at $(3\frac{1}{2}, 2\frac{1}{4})$?

    a. R

    b. T

    c. V

    d. W

27. Curtis measured the temperature of water in a flask in Science class. The temperature of the water was 35°C. He carefully heated the flask so that the temperature of the water increased about 2°C every 3 minutes. About how much had the temperature of the water increased after 20 minutes?

    a. 10°C

    b. 15°C

    c. 35°C

    d. 50°C

28. Carlos helped in the library by putting new books on the shelves. Each shelf held between 21 and 24 books. Each bookcase had 5 shelves and Carlos filled 2 of the bookcases. Which number is nearest to the number of books Carlos put on the shelves?
   a. 100
   b. 195
   c. 215
   d. 240

29. Denise is decorating a lamp shade. The bottom of the shade is circular and she wants to add fringe around the bottom. The diameter of the lamp shade is about 11 inches. If the fringe costs $1 per inch, about how much will all of the fringe Denise needs cost?
   a. $25
   b. $36
   c. $33
   d. $28

30. Several angles and a protractor are shown in this drawing.

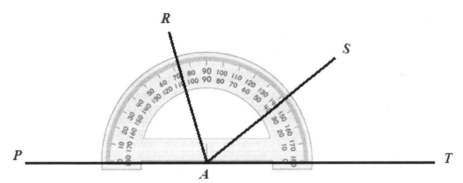

Which measure, in degrees, is closest to the measure of ∠PAS?
   a. 37°
   b. 43°
   c. 143°
   d. 157°

31. The distance from Miriam's home to her aunt's house is 27 kilometers. What is that distance in meters?
   a. 270 meters
   b. 2,700 meters
   c. 27,000 meters
   d. 27,000,000 meters

32. A lamp Sara decided to order online comes in four colors: brown, tan, white, and yellow. The shade for the lamp can be one of two styles: round or square. Which list shows all the possible combinations for a lamp of one color and one style for its shade that Sara can order?

    a. Brown, round   White, square
       Tan, round   Yellow, square
    b. Brown, tan   Yellow, round
       Tan, white   Round, square
       White, yellow
    c. Brown, tan   Tan, white
       Brown, white   Tan, round
       Brown, yellow   Tan, square
    d. Brown, round   Brown, square
       Tan, round   Tan, square
       White, round   White, square
       Yellow, round   Yellow, square

33. Alma collected coins. In the bag where she kept only dimes, she had dimes from four different years. She had 20 dimes minted in 1942, 30 minted in 1943, 40 minted in 1944, and 10 minted in 1945. If Alma reached into the bag without looking and took a dime, what is the probability that she took a dime minted in 1945?

    a. $\frac{2}{5}$

    b. $\frac{3}{10}$

    c. $\frac{1}{5}$

    d. $\frac{1}{10}$

34. People who attended an orchestra concert at Johnson Middle School were asked to which of five age groups they belonged. The data is recorded in this graph.

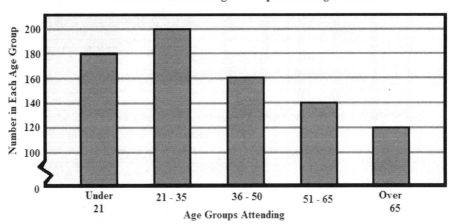

Which table correctly represents the data recorded in the graph?

a.

Number of Each Age Group Attending Concert

Age Group (in years)	Under 21	21 – 35	36 – 50	51 – 65	Over 65
Number in Group	180	200	160	140	120

b.

Number of Each Age Group Attending Concert

Age Group (in years)	Under 21	21 – 35	36 – 50	51 – 65	Over 65
Number in Group	180	220	180	160	140

c.

Number of Each Age Group Attending Concert

Age Group (in years)	Under 21	21 – 35	36 – 50	51 – 65	Over 65
Number in Group	180	200	140	120	100

d.

Number of Each Age Group Attending Concert

Age Group (in years)	Under 21	21 – 35	36 – 50	51 – 65	Over 65
Number in Group	180	200	160	120	120

35. Jacob recorded the high temperature in his backyard each day for six days. The list below shows those high temperatures.

61°, 54°, 58°, 63°, 71°, 71°

Which of these temperatures is the median of the ones in Jacob's list?

 a. 17°
 b. 62°
 c. 63°
 d. 71°

36. Mr. Smith paid $60 for a kit to build a dollhouse for his granddaughter. He also paid $10 for tools, $20 for paint, and $10 for other supplies to build the dollhouse. Which graph best represents the dollhouse expenses Mr. Smith had?

a.

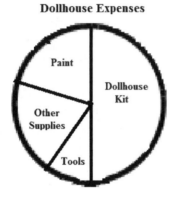

c.

b.

d.

37. The cashier at Weekender Video Arcade recorded the number of tokens sold on Thursday, Friday, Saturday, and Sunday during one weekend. The graph shows the number of tokens sold on each of those four days.

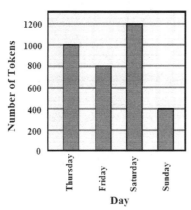

Game Tokens Sold

If the tokens sell for $1, what amount of money should the cashier have received for tokens sold on Friday and Saturday combined?
    a. $500
    b. $800
    c. $1,200
    d. $2,000

38. Harlan plans to make stew for a large group. The recipe he uses requires 150 carrots. He knows that he can buy large bags of carrots for $3.75 each. What additional information does Harlan need to find the amount of money the carrots will cost for his stew?
    a. The amounts of other vegetables he will need for the stew
    b. The number of people he expects to eat the stew
    c. The price each person attending the event paid
    d. The number of carrots in a large bag of carrots

39. Place your answer on the provided griddable sheet.
At the park, a canoe can be rented for $6 for the afternoon. A rowboat can be rented for $8 for the afternoon. The cashier collected a total of $154 one afternoon renting canoes and rowboats. If 15 canoes were rented, how many rowboats were rented that afternoon?

40. Mr. Foster wants to put new carpet on the floor of his rectangular playroom. The playroom is 27 feet long and 18 feet wide. He has found an inexpensive carpet that is priced $14 per square yard. What would be a reasonable price for enough carpet to cover the floor of his playroom?
    a. $486
    b. $756
    c. $1,260
    d. $2,268

41. Tanisha bought 6 new binders for school and paid $4 for each binder. A few days later, she saw the same binders on sale at another store for 2 for $6. How much money could Tanisha have saved if she had bought the binders at the store where they went on sale?
   a. $6
   b. $7
   c. $15
   d. $18

42. The rectangular floor of a garage has an area of 198 square feet. Andy knows that the floor is 7 feet longer than it is wide. What is length of the floor of the garage?
   a. 11 feet
   b. 14 feet
   c. 18 feet
   d. 92 feet

43. Delmon is painting a wooden fence. He painted the first board red, the second board white, and the third board blue. He continued painting the boards the same three colors, in the same order. What color did he paint the 23rd board?
   a. Red
   b. White
   c. Blue
   d. Color cannot be determined

44. Kenneth needs to repaint a wall in his bathroom. The wall is 8 feet high and 14 feet long. Part of the wall is covered with tile and he will not paint that part. The part of the wall covered by tile is 14 feet long and 42 inches high. Which expression could Kenneth use to find the area of the part of the wall he needs to repaint?
   a. $14 \times 8 - (42 + 8)$
   b. $14 \times 8 - (42 \times 14)$
   c. $14 \times 8 - [(42 \div 12) \times 14]$
   d. $2(14 + 8) - [(42 \div 12) + 14]$

45. In a new apartment building being built, it was decided that only numbers in both of the following lists would be given as apartment numbers. Both lists increase arithmetically.
   List 1: 2, 5, 8, 11, 14, ...
   List 2: 1, 5, 9, 13, 17, ...
Which of the following sets of numbers contain three numbers which can be given as apartment numbers in the new building?
   a. 5, 17, 23
   b. 5, 17, 29
   c. 17, 29, 37
   d. 17, 29, 43

46. Arlene had a garden for flowers. The rectangular garden was 10 feet wide and 16 feet long. In the garden, she planted daisies in a rectangular plot 5 feet wide and 10 feet long. She also planted pansies in a square plot 6 feet on each side. If Arlene planted no other flowers, how much area in her garden could still be planted?

    a. 13 square feet, because $2(10 + 16) – [2(5 + 10)+ 2(6 + 6)] = 13$

    b. 38 square feet, because $2(10 + 16) – (5 \times 10) + (6 \times 6) = 38$

    c. 74 square feet, because $10 \times 16 – [(5 \times 10) + (6 \times 6)] = 74$

    d. 146 square feet, because $10 \times 16 – (5 \times 100) + (6 \times 6) = 146$

47. There are five points labeled on this grid.

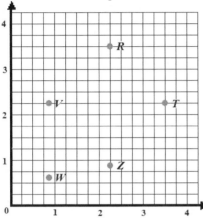

Which of the coordinates on the grid best represents the point R?

    a. $(3\frac{1}{2}, 2\frac{1}{2})$

    b. $(2\frac{1}{4}, 3\frac{1}{2})$

    c. $(3\frac{1}{2}, 4\frac{1}{2})$

    d. $(2\frac{1}{4}, 3\frac{1}{4})$

48. Place your answer on the provided griddable sheet.
The soccer field was 30 yards long. What is that distance in feet?

49. The merry-go-round is approximately 20 feet across. Which of these is closest to the distance around the merry-go-round?

    a. 20 feet

    b. 60 feet

    c. 40 feet

    d. 10 feet

50. *Place your answer on the provided griddable answer sheet.*
Marjorie collected the ages of her friends. What is the range of her friends' ages?

                10, 12, 8, 7, 14, 10, 11, 9

51. Victor played a game which used a fair spinner like the one shown here. Victor needs the arrow to land on red on his next turn.

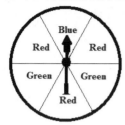

What is the probability that the arrow lands on red when Victor spins one time?

a. $\frac{1}{6}$

b. $\frac{1}{3}$

c. $\frac{1}{2}$

d. $\frac{2}{3}$

52. Xander was given 10 cups of birdfeed to pour into four birdfeeders. He poured 2 cups of feed into one feeder, 4 cups of feed into the second feeder, 2 cups of feed into the third feeder, and 1 cup into the fourth feeder. He did not put birdfeed anywhere else. Which expression best represents the amount of birdfeed leftover after Xander poured birdfeed into the four birdfeeders?

a. 10 + 2 + 4 + 2 + 1
b. 2 + 4 + 2 + 1 -10
c. 4 – 10 + 2 + 2 +1
d. 10 – 2 – 4 – 2 - 1

Answers and Explanations

TEKS Standard §111.26(b)(2)(D)

1. D: To correctly order the numbers in this question, making the decimals all have the same number of digits by adding as many zeros as necessary to the numbers with fewer digits makes them easier to compare. Here, only 17.4 has fewer digits than the others, so add one zero to make it 17.40 (*this does not change the value*). Now, by comparing place values from left to right of 17.03, 17.4, 17.31, and 17.09, we see that 17.03 is the shortest, 17.09 is the next longest, 17.31 is the third longest, and 17.4 is the longest. Notice the question asked for shortest to longest, not longest to shortest.

TEKS Standard §111.26(b)(4)(E)

2. A: In order to answer this question, we add the number of baseball and football cards to realize that there are 50 total cards in Castor's collection, 40 of which are baseball cards. To convert this to a decimal, we need to divide 40 by 50. This gives the correct answer, 0.8.

TEKS Standard §111.26(b)(7)(A)

3. C: There is more than one way to solve this problem. One method is to use the fact that the number ends in 0. This means 10 is a factor. So, 10 × 63 = 630. 10 has prime factors of 2 and 5. 63 has factors of 7 and 9 and the 9 has two factors of 3. Putting the prime factors in order, least to greatest, and showing the two factors of 3 with an exponent of 2 gives us the answer: $2 \times 3^2 \times 5 \times 7$.

TEKS Standard §111.26(b)(2)

4. The correct answer is 30. There is more than one way to solve this problem. One method is to find the greatest common factor of 150, 180, and 240. First, find the prime factors of each number.
150 = 2 × 3 × 5 × 5
180 = 2 × 2 × 3 × 3 × 5
240 = 2 × 2 × 2 × 2 × 3 × 5
Notice that the factors common to all three numbers are 2, 3, and 5. Multiply 2 × 3 × 5 to get 30, the greatest common factor. This means that the principal can make 30 groups that have the same number of students from each grade.

TEKS Standard §111.26(b)(2) and (7)(A)

5. B: There is more than one way to solve this problem. One method is to find the least common multiple of 60 and 80. To do this, first find the prime factors of each number.
60 = 2 × 2 × 3 × 5
80 = 2 × 2 × 2 × 2 × 5
The factors common to 60 and 80 are 2, 2, and 5. The factors that are not common to both numbers are two factors of 2 from 80 and a factor of 3 from 60. To find the least common multiple, multiply all the factors without repetition. That is, multiply the common factors (2, 2, and 5) and the other factors (2, 2, and 3) together:
2 × 2 × 2 × 2 × 3 × 5 = 240
240 is the least common multiple. This is the total number of beads needed of each color. To find how many bags the club will need to purchase, divide this total by the number of beads that come in each bag for each color bead. 240 ÷ 60 = 4 (4 bags of blue). 240 ÷ 80 = 3 (3 bags of silver).

TEKS Standard §111.26(b)(5)

6. C: To answer this question, notice that this figure is a regular hexagon, having 6 equal sides and angles. The part painted darker can be represented by $\frac{1}{6}$. The part painted lighter is clearly $\frac{1}{2}$, which is equivalent to $\frac{3}{6}$. The whole figure is represented by the number 1. So, 1 minus $\frac{1}{6}$ minus $\frac{3}{6}$ equals $\frac{2}{6}$ which is equivalent to $\frac{1}{3}$. Therefore, the equation, $1 - \frac{1}{6} - \frac{1}{2} = \frac{1}{3}$ best models the part of the figure Olga left white.

TEKS Standard §111.26(b)(3)

7. D: To answer this question, note that the fractions have common denominators. When adding fractions with common denominators, we need to add only the numerators, so, the sum of $\frac{6}{10}$ and $\frac{8}{10}$ is $\frac{14}{10}$. This should then be written as a mixed number, $1\frac{4}{10}$, which is found by dividing 14 by 10 which gives the whole number and the remainder becomes your new numerator over the same denominator of 10. The fraction $\frac{4}{10}$ can also be written as $\frac{2}{5}$ by dividing numerator and denominator by the common factor of 2. Therefore, $\frac{14}{10}$ is equivalent to $1\frac{2}{5}$. Be careful here to remember the 1 from the original $1\frac{6}{10}$ amount given in the problem, which must be added to the $1\frac{2}{5}$ to make a total of $2\frac{2}{5}$.

TEKS Standard §111.26(b)(3)

8. C: First, multiply the cost of each tire, $144, by the number of tires, 8, to get $1,152. Then, divide $1,152 by the number of months, 18, to get the amount paid each month, $64.

TEKS Standard §111.26(b)(1)(B) and (1)(C) and (3)

9. B: 3,700 is the only answer between the minimum number of potatoes that could have been on the trailer, 150 X 23= 3,450, and the maximum number of potatoes that could have been on the trailer, 27 X 150 = 4,050. Another method that could be used to answer this question is to multiply 25, the number halfway between 23 and 27, by 150. The product, 3,750 is very near the correct answer.

TEKS Standard §111.26(b)(3)

10. B: To simplify this expression, use the order of operations. First, do what is in the parenthesis and subtract 1 from 3 to get 2. Then, we multiply 4 times 2 to get 8. Last, subtract the 8 from 40 to get 32.

TEKS Standard §111.26(b)(4)

11. A: The ratio asked for is the number of finches compared to the number of sparrows. This compares 16 to 20, but the ratio can be written in simpler form by dividing both numbers in the ratio by 4, to get the ratio of 4 to 5. It is important to notice the order of the ratio. Since the number of finches is written before the number of sparrows, the ratio must be 16 to 20 and not 20 to 16. Also, note that the number of wrens or jays does not matter here.

TEKS Standard §111.26(b)(4)

12. C: The ratio compares the number of coffee drinkers to the number of tea drinkers, in that order, so the ratio is 45 to 20. Note that the ratio of 20 to 45 would be incorrect. The ratio of 45 to 20 can then be written in simpler terms by dividing both terms by 5 to get 9 to 4. Notice that the number of hot chocolate drinkers is not important in this problem.

TEKS Standard §111.26(b)(4)(G)

13. C: The 80% means 80 out of 100, which can be written as $\frac{80}{100}$. This fraction can be written in lowest terms by dividing both the numerator and denominator by the greatest common factor of 20, to get the fraction, $\frac{4}{5}$.

TEKS Standard §111.26(b)(4)(F)

14. D: The number of shaded parts is 8 and the total number of parts is 10. This can be written as the ratio: $\frac{8}{10}$. Since percent is always a ratio with a denominator of 100, multiply both terms of the ratio by 10 to get the ratio: $\frac{80}{100}$, which can be written as 80%.

TEKS Standard §111.26(b)(4)(C)

15. B: One method that can be used to answer this question is to write and solve the proportion: $\frac{3}{20} = \frac{V}{360}$, where V stands for the number of Brand V televisions that were sold at the furniture store. To solve the proportion, we can cross multiply: 20 times V and 3 times 360, which gives the equation: $20V = 1,080$. We solve this equation by dividing both sides of the equation by 20 to get $V = 54$.

TEKS Standard §111.26(b)(2)

16. C: Notice that there is a difference of 5 between the values in Column 2. This gives the "5" in front of n. Then, notice that if you multiply the position of the term by 5, the value is less than that product, by 4. So, the rule is $5n - 4$.

TEKS Standard §111.26(b)(1)(D) and (3)

17. B: There is a one-time charge of $50 for the price of the phone and a $45 monthly charge in the first month for a total of $95. Then, a charge of $45 only is added for every month after that. Since the chart shows the total charge each month, adding $45 to the total due from the first month gives a total of $140 for the first 2 months. Then, $45 is added for the next month, for a total of $185 for the first 3 months, $230 for 4 months, $275 for 5 months, and $320 in total charges for the first 6 months.

TEKS Standard §111.26(b)(8)(C)

18. D: The formula for the area of a triangle can be used here, but it is not necessary. To find the relationship between the heights and areas, look at the last two rows. A pattern can be seen that each value for the area, A, is just 15 times the value of the height, h. So, the formula is: $A = 15h$.

TEKS Standard §111.26(b)(9)

19. B: The amount charged for hours worked will require us to multiply the number of hours by $65. The charge for parts is not changed by the number of hours worked. So, the

equation needs to show 65 times h, the number of hours, plus p, the price of the parts. So, the correct equation is: $c = 65h + p$.

TEKS Standard §111.26(b)(8)

20. B: An acute angle measures between 0 and 90 degrees and $\angle P$ is the only choice which has a measure between 0 and 90 degrees.

TEKS Standard §111.26(b)(8)

21. D: An obtuse angle has a measure between 90 and 180 degrees and $\angle Y$ is the only angle with a measure in that range.

TEKS Standard §111.26(b)(8)(A)

22. D: To find $m\angle W$, we must first find the measure of $\angle X$. We know $m\angle X$ is 50° more than $m\angle V$. Since $m\angle V = 20°$, then $m\angle X = 20° + 50° = 70°$. So, $m\angle V + m\angle X = 90°$. It is important here to know that the sum of the three angles of any triangle is 180°. Since $m\angle V + m\angle X = 90°$, then $90° + m\angle W = 180°$. So, $m\angle W = 90°$.

TEKS Standard §111.26(b)(8)

23. C: Since we are told that $m\angle N$ is 4 times $m\angle K$, we can find the $m\angle N$ by multiplying 36° by 4 to get 144°. Knowing $\angle M$ measures 36° because it is equal to $m\angle K$ gives us the measures of three of the angles. The sum of the four angles of a quadrilateral always equals 360°. So, we add the measures of the three angles that we know and then subtract that total from 360°: 360 – (36 + 144 +36) = 360 – 216 = 144. The measure of $\angle L$ is 144°.

TEKS Standard §111.26(b)(8)

24. A: The distance given from the top to the bottom of the tire through the center is the diameter. Finding the distance the bike traveled in one complete roll of the tire is the same as finding the circumference. Using the formula, $C = \pi d$, we multiply 27 by π. From the first mark to the fourth, the tire rolls three times, so we now multiply by 3.

TEKS Standard §111.26(b)(8)

25. D: The formula for finding the circumference of a circle is: $C = 2\pi r$. The 16 in this drawing is the radius. So, to find the length of the circle, we must multiply 2 times 16 times π. Since she must also paint the length of the radius, the best expression for this total length is $2(16\pi) + 16$.

TEKS Standard §111.26(b)(11)

26. B: Each of the units represents $\frac{1}{4}$. The point T is 14 units right of the $y-$ axis or $\frac{14}{4}$ units, which is equivalent to $3\frac{1}{2}$. The point T is also 9 units from the $x-$ axis, or $\frac{9}{4}$, which is equivalent to $2\frac{1}{4}$. Be careful to notice that coordinate pairs always come in the order of the x-coordinate and then the y-coordinate, which is why Point R would be incorrect.

TEKS Standard §111.26(b)(3)(D)

27. B: Since the water temperature increased by about 2° every 3 minutes, we need to divide the total time of 20 minutes by 3 minutes, which is about 7. This means the temperature was raised about 7 times. Then we need to multiply 7 by 2, since the temperature went up by 2° each time. So, the temperature goes up by about 14° total. Since the problem asks for the increase in temperature and not the total temperature that results after the increases, 15 is the closest to our answer.

TEKS Standard §111.26(b)(3)(D)

28. C: First, since there are 5 shelves on each of the 2 bookcases, we multiply 5 by 2 to get 10 shelves total. Then, we find the minimum and maximum number of books that could have filled the shelves. Since 21 times 10 is 210 and 24 times 10 is 240, The number of books he shelved must be between 210 and 240. Answer D is 240, which would mean that every shelf was filled with the maximum number of books, which is not as likely.

TEKS Standard §111.26(b)(3) and (8)

29. C: The distance around the bottom of the lamp shade is the circumference. To find the circumference, we use the formula, $C = \pi d$. So, we must multiply 11 by π. Since 3 is close to the value of π, we can multiply 11 by 3 to find a number close to the circumference. That number is 33 inches, and at $1 per inch, 33 times $1 is $33.

TEKS Standard §111.26(b)(8)

30. C: Since segment PA lies along the left side of the protractor, we should read the outside scale. The segment SA passes between 140° and 150°, much closer to 140°, so the correct answer is 143°.

TEKS Standard §111.26(b)(4)(H)

31. C: There are 1,000 meters in every kilometer. Since we are converting from a larger unit to a smaller unit, we should multiply the number of the larger unit by the conversion factor. That gives us 27 times 1,000, which equals 27,000.

TEKS Standard §111.26(b)(12)

32. D: This list is the only one which lists all the possible ways Sara can order the lamp. Each of the four color choices can be chosen, and they can all be combined with one of two styles. In total, there are eight possibilities.

TEKS Standard §111.26(b)(12)

33. D: By adding all of the dimes, we find that there are a total of 100 dimes in the bag. 10 of them were minted in 1945. The probability, then, of choosing a dime minted in 1945 is 10 out of 100, which is equivalent to the fraction $\frac{1}{10}$.

TEKS Standard §111.26(b)(12)(A)

34. A: This table is the only one with the correct numbers from the graph for each category.

TEKS Standard §111.26(b)(12)(C)

35. B: To find the median of a set of data, first arrange the numbers in numerical order. Since this is an even numbered list, the two most central numbers are 61 and 63. Midway between these numbers is 62.

TEKS Standard §111.26(b)(12)(A)

36. D: By adding up all of Mr. Smith's expenses for the dollhouse, $60 + $10 + $20 + $10, you find that his expenses totaled $100. Mr. Smith spent $60 on the kit, which is more than $\frac{1}{2}$ his expenses ($\frac{1}{2}$ of $100 would be $50), $\frac{1}{10}$ of his expenses on tools ($\frac{1}{10}$ of $100 = $10), $\frac{1}{5}$ of his expenses on paint ($\frac{1}{5}$ of $100 = $20), and $\frac{1}{10}$ of his expenses on other supplies. This is the only graph that correctly shows these fractions.

TEKS Standard §111.26(b)(13)(A)

37. D: Though the graph shows the numbers of tokens sold on Thursday through Sunday, we are only asked about those sold on Friday and Saturday. So, we add those numbers together to get 800 + 1,200 = 2,000. Then, since each of the 2,000 tokens sold for $1 each, the 2,000 should be multiplied by $1 to get $2000.

TEKS Standard §111.26(b)(1)(B)

38. D: Since Harlan knows the cost of each bag of carrots, and also how many total carrots he needs, he also needs to know the number of carrots in each bag to find the number of bags he needs to buy. Then, he can multiply the number of bags by the price to find the amount of money the carrots for his stew will cost.

TEKS Standard §111.26(b)(3)

39. The correct answer is 8. To find the answer to this question, first find the total amount of money spent to rent 15 canoes. Multiply 15 times $6 to get $90. The remainder of the $154 that was spent on both canoes and rowboats is the amount spent on rowboats, so $154 – $90 is $64. Then we divide $64 by $8 (the price to rent a rowboat) to get 8, which is the number of rowboats rented.

TEKS Standard §111.26(b)(4)(H) and (8)(D)

40. B: It is necessary to find the area of the floor by multiplying the dimensions together. However, since the dimensions are given in feet and we only know the price of carpeting per square yard, converting the dimensions from feet to yards first is helpful. Since there are 3 feet in a yard, dividing each of the dimensions by 3 will give us the measurements in yards. So, 18/3 = 6 and 27/3 = 9. So, the floor is 6 yards by 9 yards, which is an area of 54 square yards. Last, we multiply 54 by $14, since each square yard costs $14 and there are 54, so the price of the carpet should be $756.

TEKS Standard §111.26(b)(3)

41. A: To find the answer, first determine the amount the binders cost at the different stores. At the first store, the price would be 6 times $4, since each binder costs $4, which is $24. At the second store, the binders are sold in twos. 6 binders would be 3 pairs of binders, and since each pair costs $6, $6 times 3 is the total cost of the binders at the second store, which is $18. We then subtract to find the difference, $24 - $18 = $6.

TEKS Standard §111.26(b)(8)(D)

42. C: Guess and check is one way to find the correct answer. We know the length times the width gives the area of the garage floor, 198 square feet. We might guess that the width is 9. We know that the length is 7 more than the width, so, then the length would be 16. 9 times 16 is 144. We would see that our first guess is too low, so we guess higher. We might guess 12 for the width. The length is 7 more, so the length would be 19. 12 times 19 is 228, but this is too high. When we try 11 for the width, we find the length to be 18. 11 times 18 is

198, so the width of the garage floor is 11 and the length is 18. Be careful to note that the question asks for the length and not the width.

TEKS Standard §111.26(b)(2)

43. B: This pattern repeats in groups of 3. The multiples of 3 are all painted blue because that is the third color (3, 6, 9, 12, ...). The number 23 is not a multiple of 3; it is one less than 24, a multiple of 3. The boards located one left of the boards that are multiples of 3 are painted white.

TEKS Standard §111.26(b)(8)(C)

44. C: We multiply the length and wide of the wall to find the area of the entire wall. So, 8 × 14. Then, we want to subtract the area of the tiled section that does not need to be painted from the area of the entire wall. However, the height of the tiled section is given in inches, while all the other dimensions in the problem are given in feet. So, we must convert this to feet. Since we are going from a smaller unit to a larger unit (inches to feet), we want to divide. We need to divide 42 by 12 since that is the conversion factor (12 inches in 1 foot). Then we multiply the height (in feet) by the length to find the area covered by the tile. So, this is 14 times the 42 divided by 12. Last, we subtract the two areas to find the area of the part of the wall Kenneth will repaint.

TEKS Standard §111.26(b)(2)

45. B: Since the first list increases by 3's and the second list by 4's, this means that the apartment numbers together increase by 12's (3 times 4). Since the two lists begin at different values, it is important to note that 5 is the first apartment number the two lists have in common. So, the set of numbers which can be apartment numbers can be found by increasing arithmetically by 12 starting at 5: 5, 17, 29, 41, 53, 65, ... The numbers 5, 17, and 29 are all in both lists.

TEKS Standard §111.26(b)(8)(D)

46. C: The area of the garden should be found by multiplying 10 times 16 to get 160. Then the area of the daisy plot can be found by multiplying 5 times 10 to get 50, and the area of the pansy plot can be found by multiplying 6 times 6 to get 36. We then add the 50 square feet and 36 square feet to get 86 square feet, which is the area the two plots (daisy and pansy) cover. To find the area of the garden that can still be planted, subtract that from the total area of 160 square feet to get 74 square feet.

TEKS Standard §111.26(b)(11)

47. B: Each of the units represents $\frac{1}{4}$. The point R is 9 units to the right of the $y-$ axis or $\frac{9}{4}$, which is equivalent to $2\frac{1}{4}$. Point R is also 14 units above the $x-$ axis or $\frac{14}{4}$, which is equivalent to $3\frac{1}{2}$. Be careful to notice that coordinate pairs always come in the order of the x-coordinate and then the y-coordinate.

TEKS Standard §111.26(b)(4)(H)

48. The answer is 90. There are 3 feet in every yard; therefore this is a simple multiplication problem. 30 yards X 3 feet/yard = 90 feet.

TEKS Standard §111.26(b)(8)

49. B: The distance across the merry-go-round that is given is the diameter of the ride. The distance around the merry-go-round is the circumference. To find the circumference, multiply the diameter, 20 feet, by π. Since 3 is fairly close to the value of π, 20 times 3 gives 60 feet.

TEKS Standard §111.26(b)(12)(C)

50. The correct answer is 7. Begin by arranging the different ages from least to greatest:
$$7, 8, 9, 10, 10, 11, 12, 14$$
Range is the difference between the highest and lowest values in a set of data; therefore, $14 - 7 = 7$.

TEKS Standard §111.26(b)(12)

51. C: There are 3 red sections on the spinner and the spinner has 6 sections in all. The probability of spinning red is 3 out of 6, when expressed as a fraction is $\frac{3}{6}$. Written in simplest terms, the fraction is $\frac{1}{2}$.

TEKS Standard §111.26(b)(3)(D)

52. D: Only answer D correctly shows each amount of birdfeed being subtracted from the original total amount of 10 cups that originally given to Xander.

Secret Key #1 - Time is Your Greatest Enemy

Pace Yourself

Wear a watch. At the beginning of the test, check the time (or start a chronometer on your watch to count the minutes), and check the time after every few questions to make sure you are "on schedule."

If you are forced to speed up, do it efficiently. Usually one or more answer choices can be eliminated without too much difficulty. Above all, don't panic. Don't speed up and just begin guessing at random choices. By pacing yourself, and continually monitoring your progress against your watch, you will always know exactly how far ahead or behind you are with your available time. If you find that you are one minute behind on the test, don't skip one question without spending any time on it, just to catch back up. Take 15 fewer seconds on the next four questions, and after four questions you'll have caught back up. Once you catch back up, you can continue working each problem at your normal pace.

Furthermore, don't dwell on the problems that you were rushed on. If a problem was taking up too much time and you made a hurried guess, it must be difficult. The difficult questions are the ones you are most likely to miss anyway, so it isn't a big loss. It is better to end with more time than you need than to run out of time.

Lastly, sometimes it is beneficial to slow down if you are constantly getting ahead of time. You are always more likely to catch a careless mistake by working more slowly than quickly, and among very high-scoring test takers (those who are likely to have lots of time left over), careless errors affect the score more than mastery of material.

Secret Key #2 - Guessing is not Guesswork

You probably know that guessing is a good idea - unlike other standardized tests, there is no penalty for getting a wrong answer. Even if you have no idea about a question, you still have a 20-25% chance of getting it right.

Most test takers do not understand the impact that proper guessing can have on their score. Unless you score extremely high, guessing will significantly contribute to your final score.

Monkeys Take the Test

What most test takers don't realize is that to insure that 20-25% chance, you have to guess randomly. If you put 20 monkeys in a room to take this test, assuming they answered once per question and behaved themselves, on average they would get 20-25% of the questions correct. Put 20 test takers in the room, and the average will be much lower among guessed questions. Why?
    1. The test writers intentionally write deceptive answer choices that "look" right. A test

taker has no idea about a question, so picks the "best looking" answer, which is often wrong. The monkey has no idea what looks good and what doesn't, so will consistently be lucky about 20-25% of the time.

2. Test takers will eliminate answer choices from the guessing pool based on a hunch or intuition. Simple but correct answers often get excluded, leaving a 0% chance of being correct. The monkey has no clue, and often gets lucky with the best choice.

This is why the process of elimination endorsed by most test courses is flawed and detrimental to your performance- test takers don't guess, they make an ignorant stab in the dark that is usually worse than random.

$5 Challenge

Let me introduce one of the most valuable ideas of this course- the $5 challenge:

You only mark your "best guess" if you are willing to bet $5 on it.
You only eliminate choices from guessing if you are willing to bet $5 on it.

Why $5? Five dollars is an amount of money that is small yet not insignificant, and can really add up fast (20 questions could cost you $100). Likewise, each answer choice on one question of the test will have a small impact on your overall score, but it can really add up to a lot of points in the end.

The process of elimination IS valuable. The following shows your chance of guessing it right:

If you eliminate wrong answer choices until only this many remain:	Chance of getting it correct:
1	100%
2	50%
3	33%

However, if you accidentally eliminate the right answer or go on a hunch for an incorrect answer, your chances drop dramatically: to 0%. By guessing among all the answer choices, you are GUARANTEED to have a shot at the right answer.

That's why the $5 test is so valuable- if you give up the advantage and safety of a pure guess, it had better be worth the risk.

What we still haven't covered is how to be sure that whatever guess you make is truly random. Here's the easiest way:

Always pick the first answer choice among those remaining.

Such a technique means that you have decided, **before you see a single test question**, exactly how you are going to guess- and since the order of choices tells you nothing about which one is correct, this guessing technique is perfectly random.

This section is not meant to scare you away from making educated guesses or eliminating choices- you just need to define when a choice is worth eliminating. The $5 test, along with a pre-defined random guessing strategy, is the best way to make sure you reap all of the benefits of guessing.

Secret Key #3 - Practice Smarter, Not Harder

Many test takers delay the test preparation process because they dread the awful amounts of practice time they think necessary to succeed on the test. We have refined an effective method that will take you only a fraction of the time.

There are a number of "obstacles" in your way to succeed. Among these are answering questions, finishing in time, and mastering test-taking strategies. All must be executed on the day of the test at peak performance, or your score will suffer. The test is a mental marathon that has a large impact on your future.

Just like a marathon runner, it is important to work your way up to the full challenge. So first you just worry about questions, and then time, and finally strategy:

Success Strategy

1. Find a good source for practice tests.
2. If you are willing to make a larger time investment, consider using more than one study guide- often the different approaches of multiple authors will help you "get" difficult concepts.
3. Take a practice test with no time constraints, with all study helps "open book." Take your time with questions and focus on applying strategies.
4. Take a practice test with time constraints, with all guides "open book."
5. Take a final practice test with no open material and time limits

If you have time to take more practice tests, just repeat step 5. By gradually exposing yourself to the full rigors of the test environment, you will condition your mind to the stress of test day and maximize your success.

Secret Key #4 - Prepare, Don't Procrastinate

Let me state an obvious fact: if you take the test three times, you will get three different scores. This is due to the way you feel on test day, the level of preparedness you have, and, despite the test writers' claims to the contrary, some tests WILL be easier for you than others.

Since your future depends so much on your score, you should maximize your chances of success. In order to maximize the likelihood of success, you've got to prepare in advance. This means taking practice tests and spending time learning the information and test taking strategies you will need to succeed.

Never take the test as a "practice" test, expecting that you can just take it again if you need to. Feel free to take sample tests on your own, but when you go to take the official test, be prepared, be focused, and do your best the first time!

Secret Key #5 - Test Yourself

Everyone knows that time is money. There is no need to spend too much of your time or too little of your time preparing for the test. You should only spend as much of your precious time preparing as is necessary for you to get the score you need.

Once you have taken a practice test under real conditions of time constraints, then you will know if you are ready for the test or not.

If you have scored extremely high the first time that you take the practice test, then there is not much point in spending countless hours studying. You are already there.

Benchmark your abilities by retaking practice tests and seeing how much you have improved. Once you score high enough to guarantee success, then you are ready.

If you have scored well below where you need, then knuckle down and begin studying in earnest. Check your improvement regularly through the use of practice tests under real conditions. Above all, don't worry, panic, or give up. The key is perseverance!

Then, when you go to take the test, remain confident and remember how well you did on the practice tests. If you can score high enough on a practice test, then you can do the same on the real thing.

General Strategies

The most important thing you can do is to ignore your fears and jump into the test immediately- do not be overwhelmed by any strange-sounding terms. You have to jump into the test like jumping into a pool- all at once is the easiest way.

Make Predictions

As you read and understand the question, try to guess what the answer will be. Remember that several of the answer choices are wrong, and once you begin reading them, your mind will immediately become cluttered with answer choices designed to throw you off. Your mind is typically the most focused immediately after you have read the question and digested its contents. If you can, try to predict what the correct answer will be. You may be surprised at what you can predict.

Quickly scan the choices and see if your prediction is in the listed answer choices. If it is, then you can be quite confident that you have the right answer. It still won't hurt to check the other answer choices, but most of the time, you've got it!

Answer the Question

It may seem obvious to only pick answer choices that answer the question, but the test writers can create some excellent answer choices that are wrong. Don't pick an answer just because it sounds right, or you believe it to be true. It MUST answer the question. Once you've made your selection, always go back and check it against the question and make sure that you didn't misread the question, and the answer choice does answer the question posed.

Benchmark

After you read the first answer choice, decide if you think it sounds correct or not. If it doesn't, move on to the next answer choice. If it does, mentally mark that answer choice. This doesn't mean that you've definitely selected it as your answer choice, it just means that it's the best you've seen thus far. Go ahead and read the next choice. If the next choice is worse than the one you've already selected, keep going to the next answer choice. If the next choice is better than the choice you've already selected, mentally mark the new answer choice as your best guess.

The first answer choice that you select becomes your standard. Every other answer choice must be benchmarked against that standard. That choice is correct until proven otherwise by another answer choice beating it out. Once you've decided that no other answer choice seems as good, do one final check to ensure that your answer choice answers the question posed.

Valid Information

Don't discount any of the information provided in the question. Every piece of information may be necessary to determine the correct answer. None of the information in the question is there to throw you off (while the answer choices will certainly have information to throw you off). If two seemingly unrelated topics are discussed, don't ignore either. You can be confident there is a relationship, or it wouldn't be included in the question, and you are probably going to have to determine what is that relationship to find the answer.

Avoid "Fact Traps"

Don't get distracted by a choice that is factually true. Your search is for the answer that answers the question. Stay focused and don't fall for an answer that is true but incorrect. Always go back to the question and make sure you're choosing an answer that actually answers the question and is not just a true statement. An answer can be factually correct, but it MUST answer the question asked. Additionally, two answers can both be seemingly correct, so be sure to read all of the answer choices, and make sure that you get the one that BEST answers the question.

Milk the Question

Some of the questions may throw you completely off. They might deal with a subject you have not been exposed to, or one that you haven't reviewed in years. While your lack of knowledge about the subject will be a hindrance, the question itself can give you many clues that will help you find the correct answer. Read the question carefully and look for clues. Watch particularly for adjectives and nouns describing difficult terms or words that you don't recognize. Regardless of if you completely understand a word or not, replacing it with a synonym either provided or one you more familiar with may help you to understand what the questions are asking. Rather than wracking your mind about specific detailed information concerning a difficult term or word, try to use mental substitutes that are easier to understand.

The Trap of Familiarity

Don't just choose a word because you recognize it. On difficult questions, you may not recognize a number of words in the answer choices. The test writers don't put "make-believe" words on the test; so don't think that just because you only recognize all the words in one answer choice means that answer choice must be correct. If you only recognize words in one answer choice, then focus on that one. Is it correct? Try your best to determine if it is correct. If it is, that is great, but if it doesn't, eliminate it. Each word and answer choice you eliminate increases your chances of getting the question correct, even if you then have to guess among the unfamiliar choices.

Eliminate Answers

Eliminate choices as soon as you realize they are wrong. But be careful! Make sure you consider all of the possible answer choices. Just because one appears right, doesn't mean that the next one won't be even better! The test writers will usually put more than one good answer choice for every question, so read all of them. Don't worry if you are stuck between two that seem right. By getting down to just two remaining possible choices, your odds are now 50/50. Rather than wasting too much time, play the odds. You are guessing, but guessing wisely, because you've been able to knock out some of the answer choices that you know are wrong. If you are eliminating choices and realize that the last answer choice you are left with is also obviously wrong, don't panic. Start over and consider each choice again. There may easily be something that you missed the first time and will realize on the second pass.

Tough Questions

If you are stumped on a problem or it appears too hard or too difficult, don't waste time. Move on! Remember though, if you can quickly check for obviously incorrect answer choices, your chances of guessing correctly are greatly improved. Before you completely give up, at least try to knock out a couple of possible answers. Eliminate what you can and then guess at the remaining answer choices before moving on.

Brainstorm

If you get stuck on a difficult question, spend a few seconds quickly brainstorming. Run through the complete list of possible answer choices. Look at each choice and ask yourself, "Could this answer the question satisfactorily?" Go through each answer choice and consider it independently of the other. By systematically going through all possibilities, you may find something that you would otherwise overlook. Remember that when you get stuck, it's important to try to keep moving.

Read Carefully

Understand the problem. Read the question and answer choices carefully. Don't miss the question because you misread the terms. You have plenty of time to read each question thoroughly and make sure you understand what is being asked. Yet a happy medium must be attained, so don't waste too much time. You must read carefully, but efficiently.

Face Value

When in doubt, use common sense. Always accept the situation in the problem at face value. Don't read too much into it. These problems will not require you to make huge leaps of logic. The test writers aren't trying to throw you off with a cheap trick. If you have to go beyond creativity and make a leap of logic in order to have an answer choice answer the question, then you should look at the other answer choices. Don't overcomplicate the problem by creating theoretical relationships or explanations that will warp time or space. These are normal problems rooted in reality. It's just that the applicable relationship or explanation may not be readily apparent and you have to figure things out. Use your common sense to interpret anything that isn't clear.

Prefixes

If you're having trouble with a word in the question or answer choices, try dissecting it. Take advantage of every clue that the word might include. Prefixes and suffixes can be a huge help. Usually they allow you to determine a basic meaning. Pre- means before, post- means after, pro - is positive, de- is negative. From these prefixes and suffixes, you can get an idea of the general meaning of the word and try to put it into context. Beware though of any traps. Just because con is the opposite of pro, doesn't necessarily mean congress is the opposite of progress!

Hedge Phrases

Watch out for critical "hedge" phrases, such as likely, may, can, will often, sometimes, often, almost, mostly, usually, generally, rarely, sometimes. Question writers insert these hedge phrases to cover every possibility. Often an answer choice will be wrong simply because it leaves no room for exception. Avoid answer choices that have definitive words like "exactly," and "always".

Switchback Words

Stay alert for "switchbacks". These are the words and phrases frequently used to alert you to shifts in thought. The most common switchback word is "but". Others include although, however, nevertheless, on the other hand, even though, while, in spite of, despite, regardless of.

New Information

Correct answer choices will rarely have completely new information included. Answer choices typically are straightforward reflections of the material asked about and will directly relate to the question. If a new piece of information is included in an answer choice that doesn't even seem to relate to the topic being asked about, then that answer choice is likely incorrect. All of the information needed to answer the question is usually provided for you, and so you should not have to make guesses that are unsupported or choose answer choices that require unknown information that cannot be reasoned on its own.

Time Management

On technical questions, don't get lost on the technical terms. Don't spend too much time on any one question. If you don't know what a term means, then since you don't have a dictionary, odds are you aren't going to get much further. You should immediately recognize terms as whether or not you know them. If you don't, work with the other clues that you have, the other answer choices and terms provided, but don't waste too much time trying to figure out a difficult term.

Contextual Clues

Look for contextual clues. An answer can be right but not correct. The contextual clues will help you find the answer that is most right and is correct. Understand the context in which a phrase or statement is made. This will help you make important distinctions.

Don't Panic

Panicking will not answer any questions for you. Therefore, it isn't helpful. When you first see the question, if your mind goes blank, take a deep breath. Force yourself to mechanically go through the steps of solving the problem and using the strategies you've learned.

Pace Yourself

Don't get clock fever. It's easy to be overwhelmed when you're looking at a page full of questions, your mind is full of random thoughts and feeling confused, and the clock is ticking down faster than you would like. Calm down and maintain the pace that you have set for yourself. As long as you are on track by monitoring your pace, you are guaranteed to have enough time for yourself. When you get to the last few minutes of the test, it may seem like you won't have enough time left, but if you only have as many questions as you should have left at that point, then you're right on track!

Answer Selection

The best way to pick an answer choice is to eliminate all of those that are wrong, until only one is left and confirm that is the correct answer. Sometimes though, an answer choice may immediately look right. Be careful! Take a second to make sure that the other choices are not equally obvious. Don't make a hasty mistake. There are only two times that you should stop before checking other answers. First is when you are positive that the answer choice you have selected is correct. Second is when time is almost out and you have to make a quick guess!

Check Your Work

Since you will probably not know every term listed and the answer to every question, it is important that you get credit for the ones that you do know. Don't miss any questions through careless mistakes. If at all possible, try to take a second to look back over your answer selection and make sure you've selected the correct answer choice and haven't made a costly careless mistake (such as marking an answer choice that you didn't mean to mark). This quick double check should more than pay for itself in caught mistakes for the time it costs.

Beware of Directly Quoted Answers

Sometimes an answer choice will repeat word for word a portion of the question or reference section. However, beware of such exact duplication – it may be a trap! More than likely, the correct choice will paraphrase or summarize a point, rather than being exactly the same wording.

Slang

Scientific sounding answers are better than slang ones. An answer choice that begins "To compare the outcomes..." is much more likely to be correct than one that begins "Because some people insisted..."

Extreme Statements

Avoid wild answers that throw out highly controversial ideas that are proclaimed as established fact. An answer choice that states the "process should be used in certain situations, if..." is much more likely to be correct than one that states the "process should be discontinued completely." The first is a calm rational statement and doesn't even make a definitive, uncompromising stance, using a hedge word "if" to provide wiggle room, whereas the second choice is a radical idea and far more extreme.

Answer Choice Families

When you have two or more answer choices that are direct opposites or parallels, one of them is usually the correct answer. For instance, if one answer choice states "x increases" and another answer choice states "x decreases" or "y increases," then those two or three answer choices are very similar in construction and fall into the same family of answer choices. A family of answer choices is when two or three answer choices are very similar in construction, and yet often have a directly opposite meaning. Usually the correct answer choice will be in that family of answer choices. The "odd man out" or answer choice that doesn't seem to fit the parallel construction of the other answer choices is more likely to be incorrect.

Top 20 Test Taking Tips

1. Carefully follow all the test registration procedures
2. Know the test directions, duration, topics, question types, how many questions
3. Setup a flexible study schedule at least 3-4 weeks before test day
4. Study during the time of day you are most alert, relaxed, and stress free
5. Maximize your learning style; visual learner use visual study aids, auditory learner use auditory study aids
6. Focus on your weakest knowledge base
7. Find a study partner to review with and help clarify questions
8. Practice, practice, practice
9. Get a good night's sleep; don't try to cram the night before the test
10. Eat a well-balanced meal
11. Know the exact physical location of the testing site; drive the route to the site prior to test day
12. Bring a set of ear plugs; the testing center could be noisy
13. Wear comfortable, loose fitting, layered clothing to the testing center; prepare for it to be either cold or hot during the test
14. Bring at least 2 current forms of ID to the testing center
15. Arrive to the test early; be prepared to wait and be patient
16. Eliminate the obviously wrong answer choices, then guess the first remaining choice
17. Pace yourself; don't rush, but keep working and move on if you get stuck
18. Maintain a positive attitude even if the test is going poorly
19. Keep your first answer unless you are positive it is wrong
20. Check your work, don't make a careless mistake

Special Report: What Your Test Score Will Tell You About Your IQ

Did you know that most standardized tests correlate very strongly with IQ? In fact, your general intelligence is a better predictor of your success than any other factor, and most tests intentionally measure this trait to some degree to ensure that those selected by the test are truly qualified for the test's purposes.

Before we can delve into the relation between your test score and IQ, I will first have to explain what exactly is IQ. Here's the formula:

Your IQ = 100 + (Number of standard deviations below or above the average)*15

Now, let's define standard deviations by using an example. If we have 5 people with 5 different heights, then first we calculate the average. Let's say the average was 65 inches. The standard deviation is the "average distance" away from the average of each of the members. It is a direct measure of variability - if the 5 people included Jackie Chan and Shaquille O'Neal, obviously there's a lot more variability in that group than a group of 5 sisters who are all within 6 inches in height of each other. The standard deviation uses a number to characterize the average range of difference within a group.

A convenient feature of most groups is that they have a "normal" distribution- makes sense that most things would be normal, right? Without getting into a bunch of statistical mumbo-jumbo, you just need to know that if you know the average of the group and the standard deviation, you can successfully predict someone's percentile rank in the group.

Confused? Let me give you an example. If instead of 5 people's heights, we had 100 people, we could figure out their rank in height JUST by knowing the average, standard deviation, and their height. We wouldn't need to know each person's height and manually rank them, we could just predict their rank based on three numbers.

What this means is that you can take your PERCENTILE rank that is often given with your test and relate this to your RELATIVE IQ of people taking the test - that is, your IQ relative to the people taking the test. Obviously, there's no way to know your actual IQ because the people taking a standardized test are usually not very good samples of the general population- many of those with extremely low IQ's never achieve a level of success or competency necessary to complete a typical standardized test. In fact, professional psychologists who measure IQ actually have to use non-written tests that can fairly measure the IQ of those not able to complete a traditional test.

The bottom line is to not take your test score too seriously, but it is fun to compute your "relative IQ" among the people who took the test with you. I've done the calculations below. Just look up your percentile rank in the left and then you'll see your "relative IQ" for your test in the right hand column-

Percentile Rank	Your Relative IQ		Percentile Rank	Your Relative IQ
99	135		59	103
98	131		58	103
97	128		57	103
96	126		56	102
95	125		55	102
94	123		54	102
93	122		53	101
92	121		52	101
91	120		51	100
90	119		50	100
89	118		49	100
88	118		48	99
87	117		47	99
86	116		46	98
85	116		45	98
84	115		44	98
83	114		43	97
82	114		42	97
81	113		41	97
80	113		40	96
79	112		39	96
78	112		38	95
77	111		37	95
76	111		36	95
75	110		35	94
74	110		34	94
73	109		33	93
72	109		32	93
71	108		31	93
70	108		30	92
69	107		29	92
68	107		28	91
67	107		27	91
66	106		26	90
65	106		25	90
64	105		24	89
63	105		23	89
62	105		22	88
61	104		21	88
60	104		20	87

Special Report: What is Test Anxiety and How to Overcome It?

The very nature of tests caters to some level of anxiety, nervousness or tension, just as we feel for any important event that occurs in our lives. A little bit of anxiety or nervousness can be a good thing. It helps us with motivation, and makes achievement just that much sweeter. However, too much anxiety can be a problem; especially if it hinders our ability to function and perform.

"Test anxiety," is the term that refers to the emotional reactions that some test-takers experience when faced with a test or exam. Having a fear of testing and exams is based upon a rational fear, since the test-taker's performance can shape the course of an academic career. Nevertheless, experiencing excessive fear of examinations will only interfere with the test-takers ability to perform, and his/her chances to be successful.

There are a large variety of causes that can contribute to the development and sensation of test anxiety. These include, but are not limited to lack of performance and worrying about issues surrounding the test.

Lack of Preparation

Lack of preparation can be identified by the following behaviors or situations:

Not scheduling enough time to study, and therefore cramming the night before the test or exam
Managing time poorly, to create the sensation that there is not enough time to do everything
Failing to organize the text information in advance, so that the study material consists of the entire text and not simply the pertinent information
Poor overall studying habits

Worrying, on the other hand, can be related to both the test taker, or many other factors around him/her that will be affected by the results of the test. These include worrying about:

Previous performances on similar exams, or exams in general
How friends and other students are achieving
The negative consequences that will result from a poor grade or failure

There are three primary elements to test anxiety. Physical components, which involve the same typical bodily reactions as those to acute anxiety (to be discussed below). Emotional factors have to do with fear or panic. Mental or cognitive issues concerning attention spans and memory abilities.

Physical Signals

There are many different symptoms of test anxiety, and these are not limited to mental and emotional strain. Frequently there are a range of physical signals that will let a test taker know that he/she is suffering from test anxiety. These bodily changes can include the following:

Perspiring
Sweaty palms
Wet, trembling hands
Nausea
Dry mouth
A knot in the stomach
Headache
Faintness
Muscle tension
Aching shoulders, back and neck
Rapid heart beat
Feeling too hot/cold

To recognize the sensation of test anxiety, a test-taker should monitor him/herself for the following sensations:

The physical distress symptoms as listed above
Emotional sensitivity, expressing emotional feelings such as the need to cry or laugh too much, or a sensation of anger or helplessness
A decreased ability to think, causing the test-taker to blank out or have racing thoughts that are hard to organize or control.

Though most students will feel some level of anxiety when faced with a test or exam, the majority can cope with that anxiety and maintain it at a manageable level. However, those who cannot are faced with a very real and very serious condition, which can and should be controlled for the immeasurable benefit of this sufferer.

Naturally, these sensations lead to negative results for the testing experience. The most common effects of test anxiety have to do with nervousness and mental blocking.

Nervousness

Nervousness can appear in several different levels:

The test-taker's difficulty, or even inability to read and understand the questions on the test
The difficulty or inability to organize thoughts to a coherent form
The difficulty or inability to recall key words and concepts relating to the testing questions (especially essays)
The receipt of poor grades on a test, though the test material was well known by the test taker

Conversely, a person may also experience mental blocking, which involves:

Blanking out on test questions
Only remembering the correct answers to the questions when the test has already finished.

Fortunately for test anxiety sufferers, beating these feelings, to a large degree, has to do with proper preparation. When a test taker has a feeling of preparedness, then anxiety will be dramatically lessened.

The first step to resolving anxiety issues is to distinguish which of the two types of anxiety are being suffered. If the anxiety is a direct result of a lack of preparation, this should be considered a normal reaction, and the anxiety level (as opposed to the test results) shouldn't be anything to worry about. However, if, when adequately prepared, the test-taker still panics, blanks out, or seems to overreact, this is not a fully rational reaction. While this can be considered normal too, there are many ways to combat and overcome these effects.

Remember that anxiety cannot be entirely eliminated, however, there are ways to minimize it, to make the anxiety easier to manage. Preparation is one of the best ways to minimize test anxiety. Therefore the following techniques are wise in order to best fight off any anxiety that may want to build.

To begin with, try to avoid cramming before a test, whenever it is possible. By trying to memorize an entire term's worth of information in one day, you'll be shocking your system, and not giving yourself a very good chance to absorb the information. This is an easy path to anxiety, so for those who suffer from test anxiety, cramming should not even be considered an option.

Instead of cramming, work throughout the semester to combine all of the material which is presented throughout the semester, and work on it gradually as the course goes by, making sure to master the main concepts first, leaving minor details for a week or so before the test.

To study for the upcoming exam, be sure to pose questions that may be on the examination, to gauge the ability to answer them by integrating the ideas from your texts, notes and lectures, as well as any supplementary readings.

If it is truly impossible to cover all of the information that was covered in that particular term, concentrate on the most important portions, that can be covered very well. Learn these concepts as best as possible, so that when the test comes, a goal can be made to use these concepts as presentations of your knowledge.

In addition to study habits, changes in attitude are critical to beating a struggle with test anxiety. In fact, an improvement of the perspective over the entire test-taking experience can actually help a test taker to enjoy studying and therefore improve the overall experience. Be certain not to overemphasize the significance of the grade - know that the result of the test is neither a reflection of self worth, nor is it a measure of intelligence; one grade will not predict a person's future success.

To improve an overall testing outlook, the following steps should be tried:

Keeping in mind that the most reasonable expectation for taking a test is to expect to try to demonstrate as much of what you know as you possibly can.
Reminding ourselves that a test is only one test; this is not the only one, and there will be others.
The thought of thinking of oneself in an irrational, all-or-nothing term should be avoided at all costs.
A reward should be designated for after the test, so there's something to look forward to. Whether it be going to a movie, going out to eat, or simply visiting friends, schedule it in advance, and do it no matter what result is expected on the exam.

Test-takers should also keep in mind that the basics are some of the most important things, even beyond anti-anxiety techniques and studying. Never neglect the basic social, emotional and biological needs, in order to try to absorb information. In order to best achieve, these three factors must be held as just as important as the studying itself.

Study Steps

Remember the following important steps for studying:

Maintain healthy nutrition and exercise habits. Continue both your recreational activities and social pass times. These both contribute to your physical and emotional well being.
Be certain to get a good amount of sleep, especially the night before the test, because when you're overtired you are not able to perform to the best of your best ability.
Keep the studying pace to a moderate level by taking breaks when they are needed, and varying the work whenever possible, to keep the mind fresh instead of getting bored.
When enough studying has been done that all the material that can be learned has been learned, and the test taker is prepared for the test, stop studying and do something relaxing such as listening to music, watching a movie, or taking a warm bubble bath.

There are also many other techniques to minimize the uneasiness or apprehension that is experienced along with test anxiety before, during, or even after the examination. In fact, there are a great deal of things that can be done to stop anxiety from interfering with lifestyle and performance. Again, remember that anxiety will not be eliminated entirely, and it shouldn't be. Otherwise that "up" feeling for exams would not exist, and most of us depend on that sensation to perform better than usual. However, this anxiety has to be at a level that is manageable.

Of course, as we have just discussed, being prepared for the exam is half the battle right away. Attending all classes, finding out what knowledge will be expected on the exam, and knowing the exam schedules are easy steps to lowering anxiety. Keeping up with work will remove the need to cram, and efficient study habits will eliminate wasted time. Studying should be done in an ideal location for concentration, so that it is simple to become interested in the material and give it complete attention. A method such as SQ3R (Survey, Question, Read, Recite, Review) is a wonderful key to follow to make sure that the study habits are as effective as possible, especially in the case of learning from a textbook. Flashcards are great techniques for memorization. Learning to take good notes will mean that notes will be full of useful information, so that less sifting will need to be done to seek out what is pertinent for studying. Reviewing notes after class and then again on occasion will keep the information fresh in the mind. From notes that have been taken summary sheets and outlines can be made for simpler reviewing.

A study group can also be a very motivational and helpful place to study, as there will be a sharing of ideas, all of the minds can work together, to make sure that everyone understands, and the studying will be made more interesting because it will be a social occasion.

Basically, though, as long as the test-taker remains organized and self confident, with efficient study habits, less time will need to be spent studying, and higher grades will be achieved.

To become self confident, there are many useful steps. The first of these is "self talk." It has been shown through extensive research, that self-talk for students who suffer from test anxiety, should be well monitored, in order to make sure that it contributes to self confidence as opposed to sinking the student. Frequently the self talk of test-anxious students is negative or self-defeating, thinking that everyone else is smarter and faster, that they always mess up, and that if they don't do well, they'll fail the entire course. It is important to decreasing anxiety that awareness is made of self talk. Try writing any negative self thoughts and then disputing them with a positive statement instead. Begin self-encouragement as though it was a friend speaking. Repeat positive statements to help reprogram the mind to believing in successes instead of failures.

Helpful Techniques

Other extremely helpful techniques include:

Self-visualization of doing well and reaching goals
While aiming for an "A" level of understanding, don't try to "overprotect" by setting your expectations lower. This will only convince the mind to stop studying in order to meet the lower expectations.
Don't make comparisons with the results or habits of other students. These are individual factors, and different things work for different people, causing different results.
Strive to become an expert in learning what works well, and what can be done in order to improve. Consider collecting this data in a journal.
Create rewards for after studying instead of doing things before studying that will only turn into avoidance behaviors.
Make a practice of relaxing - by using methods such as progressive relaxation, self-hypnosis, guided imagery, etc - in order to make relaxation an automatic sensation.
Work on creating a state of relaxed concentration so that concentrating will take on the focus of the mind, so that none will be wasted on worrying.
Take good care of the physical self by eating well and getting enough sleep.
Plan in time for exercise and stick to this plan.

Beyond these techniques, there are other methods to be used before, during and after the test that will help the test-taker perform well in addition to overcoming anxiety.

Before the exam comes the academic preparation. This involves establishing a study schedule and beginning at least one week before the actual date of the test. By doing this, the anxiety of not having enough time to study for the test will be automatically eliminated. Moreover, this will make the studying a much more effective experience, ensuring that the learning will be an easier process. This relieves much undue pressure on the test-taker.

Summary sheets, note cards, and flash cards with the main concepts and examples of these main concepts should be prepared in advance of the actual studying time. A topic should never be eliminated from this process. By omitting a topic because it isn't expected to be on the test is only setting up the test-taker for anxiety should it actually appear on the exam. Utilize the course syllabus for laying out the topics that should be studied. Carefully go over the notes that were made in class, paying special attention to any of the issues that the professor took special care to emphasize while lecturing in class. In the textbooks, use the chapter review, or if possible, the chapter tests, to begin your review.

It may even be possible to ask the instructor what information will be covered on the exam, or what the format of the exam will be (for example, multiple choice, essay, free form, true-false). Additionally, see if it is possible to find out how many questions will be on the test. If a review sheet or sample test has been offered by the professor, make good use of it, above anything else, for the preparation for the test. Another great resource for getting to know the examination is reviewing tests from previous semesters. Use these tests to review, and aim to achieve a 100% score on each of the possible topics. With a few exceptions, the goal that you set for yourself is the highest one that you will reach.

Take all of the questions that were assigned as homework, and rework them to any other possible course material. The more problems reworked, the more skill and confidence will form as a result. When forming the solution to a problem, write out each of the steps. Don't simply do head work. By doing as many steps on paper as possible, much clarification and therefore confidence will be formed. Do this with as many homework problems as possible, before checking the answers. By checking the answer after each problem, a reinforcement will exist, that will not be on the exam. Study situations should be as exam-like as possible, to prime the test-taker's system for the experience. By waiting to check the answers at the end, a psychological advantage will be formed, to decrease the stress factor.

Another fantastic reason for not cramming is the avoidance of confusion in concepts, especially when it comes to mathematics. 8-10 hours of study will become one hundred percent more effective if it is spread out over a week or at least several days, instead of doing it all in one sitting. Recognize that the human brain requires time in order to assimilate new material, so frequent breaks and a span of study time over several days will be much more beneficial.

Additionally, don't study right up until the point of the exam. Studying should stop a minimum of one hour before the exam begins. This allows the brain to rest and put things in their proper order. This will also provide the time to become as relaxed as possible when going into the examination room. The test-taker will also have time to eat well and eat sensibly. Know that the brain needs food as much as the rest of the body. With enough food and enough sleep, as well as a relaxed attitude, the body and the mind are primed for success.

Avoid any anxious classmates who are talking about the exam. These students only spread anxiety, and are not worth sharing the anxious sentimentalities.

Before the test also involves creating a positive attitude, so mental preparation should also be a point of concentration. There are many keys to creating a positive attitude. Should fears become rushing in, make a visualization of taking the exam, doing well, and seeing an A written on the paper. Write out a list of affirmations that will bring a feeling of confidence, such as "I am doing well in my English class," "I studied well and know my material," "I enjoy this class." Even if the affirmations aren't believed at first, it sends a positive message to the subconscious which will result in an alteration of the overall belief system, which is the system that creates reality.

If a sensation of panic begins, work with the fear and imagine the very worst! Work through the entire scenario of not passing the test, failing the entire course, and dropping out of school, followed by not getting a job, and pushing a shopping cart through the dark alley where you'll live. This will place things into perspective! Then, practice deep breathing and create a visualization of the opposite situation - achieving an "A" on the exam, passing the entire course, receiving the degree at a graduation ceremony.

On the day of the test, there are many things to be done to ensure the best results, as well as the most calm outlook. The following stages are suggested in order to maximize test-taking potential:

Begin the examination day with a moderate breakfast, and avoid any coffee or beverages with caffeine if the test taker is prone to jitters. Even people who are used to managing caffeine can feel jittery or light-headed when it is taken on a test day. Attempt to do something that is relaxing before the examination begins. As last minute cramming clouds the mastering of overall concepts, it is better to use this time to create a calming outlook.
Be certain to arrive at the test location well in advance, in order to provide time to select a location that is away from doors, windows and other distractions, as well as giving enough time to relax before the test begins.
Keep away from anxiety generating classmates who will upset the sensation of stability and relaxation that is being attempted before the exam.
Should the waiting period before the exam begins cause anxiety, create a self-distraction by reading a light magazine or something else that is relaxing and simple.

During the exam itself, read the entire exam from beginning to end, and find out how much time should be allotted to each individual problem. Once writing the exam, should more time be taken for a problem, it should be abandoned, in order to begin another problem. If there is time at the end, the unfinished problem can always be returned to and completed.

Read the instructions very carefully - twice - so that unpleasant surprises won't follow during or after the exam has ended.

When writing the exam, pretend that the situation is actually simply the completion of homework within a library, or at home. This will assist in forming a relaxed atmosphere, and will allow the brain extra focus for the complex thinking function.

Begin the exam with all of the questions with which the most confidence is felt. This will build the confidence level regarding the entire exam and will begin a quality momentum. This will also create encouragement for trying the problems where uncertainty resides.

Going with the "gut instinct" is always the way to go when solving a problem. Second guessing should be avoided at all costs. Have confidence in the ability to do well.

For essay questions, create an outline in advance that will keep the mind organized and make certain that all of the points are remembered. For multiple choice, read every answer, even if the correct one has been spotted - a better one may exist.

Continue at a pace that is reasonable and not rushed, in order to be able to work carefully. Provide enough time to go over the answers at the end, to check for small errors that can be corrected.

Should a feeling of panic begin, breathe deeply, and think of the feeling of the body releasing sand through its pores. Visualize a calm, peaceful place, and include all of the sights, sounds and sensations of this image. Continue the deep breathing, and take a few minutes to continue this with closed eyes. When all is well again, return to the test.

If a "blanking" occurs for a certain question, skip it and move on to the next question. There will be time to return to the other question later. Get everything done that can be done, first, to guarantee all the grades that can be compiled, and to build all of the confidence possible. Then return to the weaker questions to build the marks from there.

Remember, one's own reality can be created, so as long as the belief is there, success will follow. And remember: anxiety can happen later, right now, there's an exam to be written!

After the examination is complete, whether there is a feeling for a good grade or a bad grade, don't dwell on the exam, and be certain to follow through on the reward that was promised...and enjoy it! Don't dwell on any mistakes that have been made, as there is nothing that can be done at this point anyway.

Additionally, don't begin to study for the next test right away. Do something relaxing for a while, and let the mind relax and prepare itself to begin absorbing information again.

From the results of the exam - both the grade and the entire experience, be certain to learn from what has gone on. Perfect studying habits and work some more on confidence in order to make the next examination experience even better than the last one.

Learn to avoid places where openings occurred for laziness, procrastination and day dreaming.

Use the time between this exam and the next one to better learn to relax, even learning to relax on cue, so that any anxiety can be controlled during the next exam. Learn how to relax the body. Slouch in your chair if that helps. Tighten and then relax all of the different muscle groups, one group at a time, beginning with the feet and then working all the way up to the neck and face. This will ultimately relax the muscles more than they were to begin with. Learn how to breathe deeply and comfortably, and focus on this breathing going in and out as a relaxing thought. With every exhale, repeat the word "relax."

As common as test anxiety is, it is very possible to overcome it. Make yourself one of the test-takers who overcome this frustrating hindrance.

Special Report: Retaking the Test: What Are Your Chances at Improving Your Score?

After going through the experience of taking a major test, many test takers feel that once is enough. The test usually comes during a period of transition in the test taker's life, and taking the test is only one of a series of important events. With so many distractions and conflicting recommendations, it may be difficult for a test taker to rationally determine whether or not he should retake the test after viewing his scores.

The importance of the test usually only adds to the burden of the retake decision. However, don't be swayed by emotion. There a few simple questions that you can ask yourself to guide you as you try to determine whether a retake would improve your score:

1. What went wrong? Why wasn't your score what you expected?

Can you point to a single factor or problem that you feel caused the low score? Were you sick on test day? Was there an emotional upheaval in your life that caused a distraction? Were you late for the test or not able to use the full time allotment? If you can point to any of these specific, individual problems, then a retake should definitely be considered.

2. Is there enough time to improve?

Many problems that may show up in your score report may take a lot of time for improvement. A deficiency in a particular math skill may require weeks or months of tutoring and studying to improve. If you have enough time to improve an identified weakness, then a retake should definitely be considered.

3. How will additional scores be used? Will a score average, highest score, or most recent score be used?

Different test scores may be handled completely differently. If you've taken the test multiple times, sometimes your highest score is used, sometimes your average score is computed and used, and sometimes your most recent score is used. Make sure you understand what method will be used to evaluate your scores, and use that to help you determine whether a retake should be considered.

4. Are my practice test scores significantly higher than my actual test score?

If you have taken a lot of practice tests and are consistently scoring at a much higher level than your actual test score, then you should consider a retake. However, if you've taken five practice tests and only one of your scores was higher than your actual test score, or if your practice test scores were only slightly higher than your actual test score, then it is unlikely that you will significantly increase your score.

5. Do I need perfect scores or will I be able to live with this score? Will this score still allow me to follow my dreams?

What kind of score is acceptable to you? Is your current score "good enough?" Do you have to have a certain score in order to pursue the future of your dreams? If you won't be happy with your current score, and there's no way that you could live with it, then you should consider a retake. However, don't get your hopes up. If you are looking for significant improvement, that may or may not be possible. But if you won't be happy otherwise, it is at least worth the effort.

Remember that there are other considerations. To achieve your dream, it is likely that your grades may also be taken into account. A great test score is usually not the only thing necessary to succeed. Make sure that you aren't overemphasizing the importance of a high test score.

Furthermore, a retake does not always result in a higher score. Some test takers will score lower on a retake, rather than higher. One study shows that one-fourth of test takers will achieve a significant improvement in test score, while one-sixth of test takers will actually show a decrease. While this shows that most test takers will improve, the majority will only improve their scores a little and a retake may not be worth the test taker's effort.

Finally, if a test is taken only once and is considered in the added context of good grades on the part of a test taker, the person reviewing the grades and scores may be tempted to assume that the test taker just had a bad day while taking the test, and may discount the low test score in favor of the high grades. But if the test is retaken and the scores are approximately the same, then the validity of the low scores are only confirmed. Therefore, a retake could actually hurt a test taker by definitely bracketing a test taker's score ability to a limited range.

Special Report: Additional Bonus Material

Due to our efforts to try to keep this book to a manageable length, we've created a link that will give you access to all of your additional bonus material.

Please visit http://www.mometrix.com/bonus948/staarg6math to access the information.